This book is dedicated to the many people who have been plagued by financial difficulties and struggled to overcome. It is my hope that the following pages will offer both hope and help.

To those who are struggling – there is hope that things can be done to change your present state into a welcomed future.

To those who are tired – strength is waiting to meet you as you continue to persevere.

To those who have failed- consider failure an event, not a destination. You only fail when you quit. Refuse to quit.

To my first wife Russa – we were together for 30 years and she was with me when I began working on this book. She has since passed away from Cancer but her memories I cherish forever.

To my children – through thick and thin you have been around me. I cannot thank you enough for the privilege of being called your father.

To my Lord – without whom none of this would even be possible.

Introduction

This book comes as the result of living for years with a burden on my shoulders. At the age of 19 my family talked me into buying a car with an interest rate of more than 24%. I had a job but no established credit and they felt that since we needed a car as a family, this was the way to go. What ended up happening was for a number of years I was plagued with bad and blemished credit.

Make no mistake. In our society it is very hard to function with bad credit. It hinders you being able to make large purchases such as houses and cars. Credit cards become almost impossible to obtain. And even some jobs check your credit report prior to hiring you.

I do not believe that we should center our lives on the use of credit. But when the option to have credit is removed, you limit your avenues of advancement.

This book is dedicated to all people who have had situations that have affected their ability to proceed forward. Maybe it was a layoff that threw all of your bills behind. Maybe you married someone with bad credit and now you are faced with dealing with their issues. Or maybe you are a hard working person who just never made enough to make ends meet.

I am here to tell you,"*You Can Fix It*". Although you may have had some difficult times in the past, it is still possible to overcome the stigma and limitations to enter into that place where you could be if certain things were in place. Now your journey is not the same as mine and although there may be some similarities, each of us is different. Instead, use what you can and apply it to your life and formulate your own individual plan for victory.

This book is very practical. I will share with you not only the way to assess your current situation but how to chart your own course for personal success. You will be amazed at how all things truly are possible to those who believe.

Now let's get started so that you too will "*Make Financial Adjustments for Financial Success*."

Table of Contents

Where We Are Today

Matthew 24:39 "And knew not until the flood came"

Many people today are faced with heavy challenges. The cost of living has escalated to where it takes more money to live than ever before. We now see cars that cost as much as houses have in the past. People live with mortgages that have payments of over $1500 a month. And there is virtually no industry that deals with producing consumer products which has not been affected by the state of our economy. Let's face it; it takes a lot to live.

In light of all of this, our economic way of life has been adversely affected. Personal bankruptcies are on the rise annually. People have more credit card debt than ever before. Even consumer debt is reaching record-breaking proportions. Under the burden of economic strain, families are falling apart. Both men and women feel the stain and spend a great deal of time each day dealing with earning enough to make ends meet. Financial problems are one of the top 5 reasons for separation and divorce among couples today.

When you take into consideration all of the various factors that affect our financial health, it is clear that people are supposed to be experiencing some stress today. So instead of taking the position that it should not be happening to me, we should understand it is part of the journey we call life.

The first step in fixing financial problems is to understand where we are today. Everyone is in a different place. Where do you see your self today (we will discuss this more in detail in the next chapter)? The world we live in is helping to stress out the lives of everyday people.

Most of us make more money than our parents ever did. Yet have you ever noticed that mom and dad had a house (maybe not the biggest one on the block), a car (maybe not the newest one on the block), wore nice clothes (maybe not designer), could stay together through thick and thin, a lot of times with our mom staying at home? How many of us had parents who by today's standards would not have been considered very educated?

Yet with all of this, they were probably happier than most couples today. Why? Because our parents learned the secret to contentment, *more is not necessarily better.* Although they did work hard, they understood that contentment is not found in the accumulation of things. If that were the case, those with the most toys would be the happiest. Nothing could be farther from the truth.

Contentment is found in learning to live a life where we are not guilty of perpetual complaining. I am not advocating that we should not want to do better, because that is a good goal to have. But complaining will not change where I am at; it only makes me more unbearable to live with today.

Instead, we should be grateful that things are no worse than they are.

I believe that if we examine the way of life back in the 1960's and 70's we can learn some things that will help us as we approach the world we live in today. For starters, the way of life was simpler. People simply had less and did less. Today what we need to fix is "how can I simplify my live? Who says you have to have 3 cars in the driveway? What's wrong with one or two instead? Why put yourself in a position to have to pay on multiple insurance policies, car notes, repair bills, etc.?

Now it is not that I am against having anything. I think that the mentality of our day is more and more and more. Let me ask you, how much is enough? When do you know that you have what you need (I didn't say what you want). It's like the child who goes into the candy store and if they had their way would buy up the whole store.

People today let the world at large dictate what should make them happy. Why is that? Have we as a society gotten so far away from independent thinking that people can no longer make up their own minds? I think not! Deep down, each of us knows what would make us truly happy. I challenge you today to discover for yourself what you need and should have in your life. Then go for it!

You see, you can never fix what you don't know is broke. This mentality that allows others to dictate the direction our lives should go in will break you. The weight of debt, bad credit, late payments or just knowing that you owe a lot can be overwhelming. *True freedom comes from being in control of your own destiny.* Whenever someone else dictates your destiny, you are headed for trouble.

Look around you! Don't you see people who are drowning under the bondage of debt? Yes they may have a new car in the driveway, wear new clothes and appear very successful. But underneath that stuff is someone who may just be one paycheck away from financial ruin. Just because something seems a certain way does not mean that it is. So many people are trying to keep up with the Joneses (no offense, but who are they anyway). But let's face it; the Joneses don't pay your bills. They have their own.

The truth is that debt is killing our society. Our federal government owes in the trillions (how much is that anyway). The Social Security system is in danger of being in serious trouble in the next 25 yrs. My heart goes out to those who think they will retire to Social Security in years to come because there is a good chance it won't be there. As a nation we are no longer considered the dominant economic force in the world. Other nations, with less than we have, have started to take a place in the world of high finance due to the lack of debt their country currently carries.

People are drowning in some problems. Maybe you are too. The good news is that if you are, you don't have to forever. It is possible to find your way out and to come out on top. But first, we must make an honest assessment of where we are financially.

I know this all sounds a little like gloom and doom. In reality, it is not. What I see is that unless we as a people come to some hard, cold facts about debt and our current spending habits, trouble will just creep up on us until it has us. By then, it may be too late.

So now is the time to do a little soul searching? Look at the news and see just where this world is. Examine where you are in relationship to where you want to be. Its *OK* if today is not looking too good for you. Remember, today is not tomorrow. There are brighter days ahead. We just need the wisdom today to prepare.

It is one thing for us to assess where the world is. We can even assess the condition of our neighbors and friends. But none of these will matter when it comes to your own personal financial situation. *The hardest part of fixing any financial situation is making a factual determination of where one is, regardless of what this determination may reveal.* You see, it is not uncommon for people to have no idea of where they truly are financially. And if you owe a lot of debt, the tendency is to put your head in the sand, pretending it will just go away. We hope that it is not too bad. It is like talking to someone who is addicted to something. Avoidance becomes a way of life.

There are those who are working on a job in which they love what they are doing but it just doesn't pay them enough money. *There are two fundamental steps in fixing financial problems; Increasing ones income (for what you have coming in may not be enough) and decreasing ones debts (for all debt must be controlled).* Many times people think that the answer to their problem comes with making more money so they will leave one job for another one paying 50 cents more. No, I know this may be hard to accept but *money management is more important than making money.* To whom much has been given much will be required and he who is faithful with little will be faithful with much. If we can learn to budget so that we are not foolishly spending, to save a portion of our income on a regular basis by paying ourselves first and to make wise investment decisions, then we are positioning ourselves for financial increase.

Are you a spender or a saver? Right now it has been estimated by some that the average American doesn't save much of his income. In fact, there are those in other countries who actually are better at saving than we do. Advertising in this country is geared towards making you part with your hard earned money. We want everything and we want it now! We enjoy convenience so much so that it is hard to conceive life without fax machines, cellular phones, pagers, the Internet, microwaves and computers. Now there is nothing wrong with any of these things but the way that we have grown accustomed to having this in our lives creates a subtle mindset that many are unaware of.

Spenders find themselves surrounded with stuff. If it's clothes, they may be very style conscious so their closets are full of things that are no longer fashionable. At times they may give in to impulse and so they shop because there is a sale (which by the way is one of the cleverest ways that marketers have gotten the consumer to give up their money).

They see things they just have to have no matter what the cost. Or they could be living the lie that the one who walks around with a pocket full of money is the one who has it. Nothing could be farther from the truth. *Real wealth is not determined by what is in your pocket but by the assets under your control.*

Then you have the Saver. This person may be somewhat of a miser, who penny pinches all through life putting something aside for the proverbial rainy day. Not all savers are misers, though. You have some who save for the sake of being prepared. Never save for a rainy day. What do you want, rain? No, we should save so that we can take advantage of opportunities that present themselves in the future and to handle adversity when it comes by not needing someone else to take care of it for us. It is not wrong to save but never because of fear. If you are afraid, you will probably hoard (remember Y2K?).

Now most people will be inclined to be one way or the other. As long as we avoid living in extremes, we will have a chance to turn out ok. There are times when money must be spent. Suppose you accept a new job that requires that you own a certain type of wardrobe. Well it might be both prudent and necessary to purchase the clothes that will allow you to perform your function. This is almost like an investment into your career. You may need to use debt to purchase some clothes (if time wont permit you to wait until you can pay cash) and as long as you understand this you can use debt to your advantage. Of course you would want to pay off this debt as soon as possible.

Conversely, in order to build your own personal portfolio, you will need to save. It works out real well when we can save 10% of our income. If you can generate 18% a year, you will watch your investment double every 4 years. But even if you can't save 10% you need to do something. If you spend all you have today there may be little or nothing left for tomorrow. Consider the ant who has no overseer or ruler but who knows to gather provisions in the summer (when it is able to) so that it will have something to eat on in the winter (when it will be almost impossible for the ant to find food). If insects and animals practice this principle people should do no less.

As we start off assessing ourselves we need to determine which side we tend to lean on, spender or saver. Whichever side it is, if we learn to practice balance, it can work out for our good. For you see, a wise person knows that at times you must spend, at others you must save.

The average American has no idea of how much they really owe. Yes, they know about the mortgage and the car payments, but how much do you spend on a cup of coffee each year? What about those donuts? And when we just happen to go out and spend $15 on lunch, do we really know how many times a year we do that and what it actually costs us? It is the little foxes that spoil the vine. We find ourselves spending more money than we realize because $2 here and $5 there does not mean much to us but over the course of say 15 or 20 years, it can add up to a nice tidy sum when you include the interest that money could have been generating.

Now I am not saying that it is wrong to spend this money. *But if you want to become truly free you must learn to pay attention to habits that have contributed to the bondage that you may be in.* It usually works out best when we allocate a certain amount of money towards those incidentals and then even if we don't know how many cups of coffee we purchased this month, we do know how much money we have spent based on the amount we allocated towards these types of purchases.

There are those who teach that when you are in debt and working to come out that you must discipline yourself to spending only what is necessary and give up what is not. I do understand this and in principle, I agree. But what I discovered for me is that I need to enjoy certain little pleasures along the way while I am working towards my goal of being financially free. So I might treat myself to some coffee and donuts on occasion or go purchase a sandwich that I have not had in awhile. Looking at where you are today allows you to address habits that are destructive *but we must be careful to not put ourselves in bondage as we are working to be free.* Remember, it can be fun getting out from under the bondages of debt. Life must be enjoyed today for tomorrow is not promised. So enjoy some of life's little pleasures today and be thankful that you are still alive to enjoy them.

Let me also say about today that sometimes we find ourselves in positions that we did not put ourselves in but were forced to accept the consequences. Many times people who have gone through a divorce find themselves with debt that they didn't have before. Sometimes they experience devastating losses financially that are just the result of a broken union. Or you may be the person who walked out of someone's life and left them with a lot of responsibilities that you jointly created. When these things occur, it will profit you nothing to sit around and blame yourself for these misfortunes. If at all possible, make things right when you can. *We must accept the things that we cannot change and focus on the things that we can so that they will change.* It is this forward movement towards progress that enables you to get the strength to continue. But remember, problems have a way of paralyzing us so that we are unable to do what we know we need to.

The good news is that no matter how bad or hopeless things may seem right now, just as they can get worst, they can also get better. As long as you are alive, there is hope. It does not matter what your circumstances say, what other people say or even what common sense may say. *WHAT DO YOU SAY?* In the quiet of the day what words are you speaking to yourself? In the stillness of the night, what words are keeping you up? You see, you believe you more than anyone else. Therefore it is vitally important that we speak the right words. Some may call this crazy, to talk to yourself. But out of the abundance of your heart will your mouth speak. If you want to know what you really believe, just keep paying attention to the words that are coming out of your mouth.

Words reveal what is in your heart. Words build up and tear down. We use words to build a relationship and words to tear them down. Words express "I love you" and "I hate you".

We use words to get someone to marry us and words form the foundation for those who divorce. A child who is continually told that he has potential, worth and self - value will grow up with security. Conversely, children who grow up being told they are worthless, nothing and a waste of life struggle with self - esteem. Many of the insecurities and hang ups we feel in our lives today as adults are the result of how we have allowed the words of others to shape our opinion of ourselves. *But it is not the words themselves that determine how you see yourself, but how much value you place on the person who spoke those words to you.* If you really love and respect someone, his or her words can either heal you or kill you.

We can lay the foundation to a great future. It will begin with our mouths. You will never rise above your level of confession. If you are afraid to say things like, "I am debt free." "I owe no man anything but to treat him with respect as a fellow human being." "I am abundantly supplied for, my needs are met and I'm out of debt." then you will most likely never experience any of this. It is not lying to say what we believe can come to pass in our lives. Whatever the mind can conceive, the heart believes and the mouth confess, you can achieve.

What is the importance to this kind of thinking? As we honestly examine where we are financially today, we must admit that a lot of it has to do with our level of thinking. Ask yourself, when you look at your current situation what do you see? Are you surrounded with feelings of hopelessness and helplessness? Do you believe that it cannot or will not change? Do you believe that what you are facing today you will face the rest of your life? What do you see when you look at today? Whatever it is, let me comfort you with these words; *nothing ever stays the same. All things change.*

And what is the picture you have of yesterday? Many times we are either very hard or very soft on ourselves when it comes to evaluating our past. For those who are hard come words from ourselves that tend to belittle us and attack our self-image (I was so stupid then. I made some really foolish mistakes. Everything that happened to me was my own fault.) Even if statements such as these are true (and most times they are not) being too hard on oneself poisons our present and prevents us from experiencing our future. The failures of yesterday paralyze us and keep us from reaching our full potential.

Then there are those who are too soft on their past. They find any and every excuse to justify why what happened to them was not their fault. Many start to develop a tendency to blame others. Even when the majority of fault lies somewhere else, as individuals we need to study ourselves so that we can learn from our experiences. Self-evaluations are a key to growth and necessary if we desire to make adjustments. If we never evaluate, we will never adjust and hence, never change.

Finally, what is the picture you have of your future? Do you see a brighter future? Do you see changing from someone who has nothing or just enough, to someone who

Walks in abundance and more than enough? If you can see it, you can have it, provided it will take you where you need to go. The question is, what do YOU see?

Your life today is just a snapshot. Chances are, when you wake up tomorrow, things will be different. Success is what so many are striving for but success is fleeting. Too many people are evading failure but failure isn't final. If there is one thing about life that is increasingly evident, it is that nothing stays the same. The sooner we accept that when we are accessing where we are, the easier it will be to move on.

It's much like eating a meal. If it is a good one, it brings back fond memories of past good meals. It helps us to enjoy our present as we savor each bite in our mouths, not just our hands. It gives us hope for a future that will hopefully be as good as or better than what we are experiencing right now. On the other hand, a bad meal will leave a certain taste in our mouths that we will not want to experience again. When food is bad, not only do we avoid it, we tell everyone we know to avoid it.

One of the rules of increase is *some equals more*. It is very hard to increase when you have nothing to start with. That is why the initial stages of growth are to first get your hand on seed (substance). If you were to study the lives of wealthy people you would find that they all started out with something even if it wasn't much. As it pertains to money and financial success, it isn't what you start out with that determines your level of success but what you do with what you have that makes the difference. We would call it *the effective management (stewardship) of resources.*

So look real hard and real long at the reality of your current situation. In the chapters to follow we will discuss how to create a strategy to address what you see in your present.

Making an Honest Assessment

Luke 14:28 "For which of you, intending to build a tower, sits not down first, and counts the cost, whether he has sufficient to finish it?"

It has been said that every journey begins with a single step. In order to begin, one must first start. *To get to where we believe we want to go, we must first evaluate where we are.*

Sad to say, this is the hardest part of true financial freedom. Most people just don't know where they truly are. They believe they are at one place when a careful analysis usually reveals that they spend more money than they think they do. Most people have no idea where their money goes and so where they think they are and where they truly are turns out to be two different places.

Let me say at this point that there are a lot of mixed feelings when it comes to the whole idea of budgets. Some see budgets as being too time consuming; others live strictly by them. I think it wise to say that we all should live somewhere in the middle. It is wise to know what is leaving each month. But once you have a handle on your finances, you can use a more relaxed budget. I do recommend that everyone who wishes to experience financial freedom start off by doing a budget and tracking their expenses.

Defining Financial Freedom for yourself

While we are at this stage, it would be wise to start off by defining what financial freedom to you is. To let our society tell us may mean having millions of dollars saved, retiring by age 35, spending our days in leisurely activities and showing the whole world that we are truly prosperous. But if you allow others to dictate your own definition of financial freedom you will never achieve it.

Freedom is the ability to express. A person who is free financially is not bound up by debt (although they may have some) and may not even be a millionaire. To have your bills paid, to be under no pressure financially, to have cash assets that you can get your hands on, to be able to help others, these are components of true financial freedom. Each and every one of us must come up with our own definition.

The reason you cannot let someone else define it for you is that their definition may be entirely different from yours. Let's say that someone is use to having a $100 million dollar fortune. To them, $1 million dollars may seem like chump change. But if you have never had any money to call your own and you suddenly come into $1 million, it may mean that you are "rich "for the rest of your life, provided you exercise good judgment.

Maybe to you, financially free is to have a paid for house. Maybe it's being able to buy a new automobile each year for cash. Maybe it's having 6 figures in your investment accounts. It could be earning the type of salary you envision people who are free earn.

Whatever the definition, it needs to be your own. If you adopt someone else's definition, you may never achieve it. There is nothing more self-demotivating than to have goals you never achieve. To become truly goal oriented you must have some victories under your belt. Let's face it; most of us will never come to know what it is to control huge amounts of wealth. It takes a lot of discipline to keep money (meaning it is actually easier to make money than to keep it).

So based on what you earn (your present earning capability), and what you can do (your future potential), that should dictate how you view financial freedom.

Let's say that in your lifetime you earn an average of $30,000 a year. Given the high cost of living and inflation, you will probably never save huge amounts of money. So this person must be wise with what they can get their hands on. If you enter into retirement and can generate an $18000/yr income (60% of what you earned while working) you have not done badly for yourself, especially when you consider that most retired people still need help from families and others to survive. Now this is not a lot of money but think of it in terms of what came into your hands. Can you expect to have DOUBLE your working salary in retirement? Should you expect that?

If during your lifetime you earned an average of $30,000 would it be realistic to expect to have an after retirement income of $100,000? Although this may happen it is not very likely. You would expect your income to drop during retirement. The good news is that your expenses should decrease as well so that it can all balance out.

So, create your own definition of financial freedom. Then as you progress along this path you can monitor your progress by what your ultimate goals are. These goals need to be specific and attainable. Don't hope to get everywhere you plan on coming in a short period of time. Give yourself years if need be to achieve your goal. Time will put the power of compound interest to work for you as you make investments into your future.

Paint the real picture

The second step in this assessment is *to see where you really are.* There are a couple of factors to consider here.

One, how much income do you really have coming in? Maybe you see money in addition to your regular job. That being the case, you need to include it in your overall financial plan. Maybe you work something on the side or have a way to earn $2,000 a year by doing something you have always done. Whatever the case, you need to know exactly how much money you are dealing with.

Next you need to know how much is really going out. Everyone usually spends more money than they know. Maybe you don't consider that can of pop with lunch each day for 50 cents but that is $2.50/week or $125/year or $1250 for 10 yrs or $5,000 over the

Span of a 40-year work life. Now I know I am stretching this a bit but I want to make a point. Money has a way of coming and going. We need to recognize it as it comes and see where it goes. If you want to purchase a pop each day, fine. But know beforehand how much it is really costing you (and consider more water and less pop).

Ask yourself questions such as, am I a compulsive spender or do I take time before committing to any purchase? Am I the type who feels that since I work I am entitled to what I want? Do I carry large amounts of cash in my pocket that I have a hard time accounting for? Or am I a good money manager? Do I save and spend? Do I make wise spending decisions? You need to know the answers to these questions.

Sometimes the best way to see this is to observe how others characterize your money management. Do you find people asking you for financial advice? Do you find yourself helping people when they have to make financial decisions without even realizing you are doing it? Have your past decisions worked out to be good financial decisions?

Armed with these bits of information we can now begin to explore where we want to go. You may discover that part of your struggle stems from the fact that you really don't make enough money. You see, there are really only 2 ways to grow financially. You must either reduce your expenses (what goes out) or increase your income (what comes in). You may discover that you are a good manager who just doesn't make enough money. Or you may have spending habits that cost you more money than it should.

As I have worked with families regarding their budgets I have found that a lot of times it is not a money problem we have (most families are earning more money than their parents did). We have more stuff at a much younger age. The major problem with this is that we end up with things before we have had the time to develop the maturity to handle them. Granted, things are more expensive but there is a mindset we have that our parents didn't). Our spending, as a society is, for the most part, out of control.

The best way to recover financially is to have a plan in place that will address increasing your income, reducing your debts and strengthening you management of money. This will give you the best return on your investment. You will have more and be more responsible with it. The reason is you will already know some things to do before you have the money or resources to do them.

In my own life I discovered that I did not know a lot about money management. I was always good in math at school. I was usually a few grades ahead in math each school year. I found that I had this thing with numbers. If we were driving in the car and my mother saw some advertisement with a phone number she would say, "Give me a pen. I want to write this number down." I would say to her, "mom, just say it and I will tell it to you when we get home." At first, she didn't believe me but in time she saw that I really did remember the number when we got home. But even with all this, I was bad at money management. I was never taught coming up about the wisdom needed to handle finances.

My parents were very simple people. They had a high school education and never had a checking account or credit cards. They handled all of their affairs by cash and money order. Now I am not criticizing this system; it is just that using a checking account is a better money management tool. But I had no exposure to it until I was a grown man.

As you endeavor to recover and to get on the right track, the hardest thing you will have to deal with is your way of thinking. I submit to you that unless you are willing to change what you think and to embrace the ideas that good money managers embrace, you will condemn yourself to a future without change. It is OK to create your own system of management but first you must understand the systems that are in place.

A Cash Flow Analysis

So now you have analyzed the money that comes in and where it goes going out. At this point I would recommend setting up a budget. This budget will allow you to see just how your money is being spent but more importantly it will show you the ways that it should be spent. If you can see in black and white that you are spending too much in one area (say $500 a month in eating out) it makes it that much easier to correct.

Now there are plenty of resources available to help you construct a budget. Personally, I like Larry Burkett's organization, Crown Financial Ministries in Gainesville, Ga. They are committed to assisting people in attaining financial health and the budget material is pretty complete.

Don't miss this all-important step. Once you are where you want to be financially, you can take another look at how you want to do your budget but in the beginning stages, it's important to establish controls. Winners know the value of keeping score.

To begin (if you don't have any resources at your disposal yet) follow these simple steps to get you on the road to creating your own budget;

1) Write down all the income you have coming in each month from all sources
2) Write down all the bills you have, along with their due dates
3) See if what you have coming in is more than what is going out

Forgive Yourself

Let's face it; most of us are not hot shot financial wizards. If we were, we would have spared ourselves a lot of the aggravation that comes with poor financial decisions. Many times we can point to different factors that influenced our decisions.

It is always bad to make financial decisions under pressure. Once I had a landlord who was a real jerk. I told the man that I would have the rent by Friday, which was my payday. He insisted that I get the check to him so that he would have it in his hands before Friday. I agreed to do so with the understanding that both of us knew the money would not be in the account before Friday. I would have to get paid and then go to the bank after work to deposit the check. As it so happens I got my check early that Friday and went during lunch to make the deposit.

Now mind you, the reason I told him to wait until Friday because I didn't have the money in the account to cover the check. When I made the deposit what did I discover? My balance was less than it should have been and that I had been assessed a bounce charge. Why? *Because Mr. Landlord deposited the check early.* So now I had less to work with than I had originally anticipated and I was already short.

Needless to say when I got home he called and was furious. Why did I give him a bad check? I politely informed him that we discussed my situation extensively prior to his receiving the check. Still, he was looking for someone to blame.

This taught me that no one knows or cares about my financial situation more than me. I am the only one who can realistically tell when I will or will not have money. From that time forward I have not put myself into a position where someone else can determine what happens with my money. As much as I can, I strive to be in control of my own personal finances and financial destiny.

Why am I telling you this? If you want to fix your current situation and grow into the situation you have dreamed of, you had better get control of your money. Don't let other people dictate to you what you will and will not have. This is my problem with working on a job and having the employer feel like they determine your worth. No, your contribution to the organization determines your worth; it is not their decision. And your family may suffer the consequences of them not paying you based on your contribution.

Everyone needs room financially to mess up. You may miss the opportunity to purchase a hot stock when it is at a real low price and now, you can't afford to get in. Maybe it was that real estate deal of the century that you didn't pursue because you were afraid. Or maybe it was that job you decided not to take which would have turned your whole financial situation around.

Whatever the case, IT'S TOO LATE NOW! So forgive yourself. Where you are is where you are and there is not a whole lot you can do to change where you have come from. The only thing that is within your power is to affect where you go from right now. This is your day. The question is what are you going to do with it?

What Now

We have been talking about making an honest assessment. There must be a place for understanding how to deal with failure in that assessment. Yes we need to forgive ourselves for past mistakes. *We must learn how to use failure as a springboard for the success that waits ahead of us.*

The difference between very successful people, those who are mediocre, and those who amount to very little in this life is tied in to how each one deals with failure. Everyone will fail. No matter how good the idea is, no matter how much research is done beforehand or how much preparation goes into getting ready for any venture, nothing works all the time. Successful people understand that failure is not final. They use it as a learning experience and learn what not to do. They try and try and try again. This develops within them a stick to it type of attitude that ultimately makes them people who are able to handle adversity.

Mediocre people see failure as something that is just a way of life. Many times they have the attitude that "you win a few, you loose a few." This causes them to accept the consequences of failure as unavoidable. *When you are dealing with financial issues it is important that you don't just take what comes.* Sometimes you have to make what you want come to you. You do this by not accepting a "no" from a lender as final. Where one lender may not give you a loan, another one may. You don't look at the money you may be earning from your job and see it as the most you could ever earn. Instead, you look for opportunities and position yourself to be ready for them when they come.

In the financial arena it all depends on who you are talking to. There are those lenders who are very strict with their policies regarding borrowing money and unless you fit perfectly into the mold they have established, you will not be approved. Then there are those lenders that I call *common sense lenders*. They make loans based on if they make prudent financial sense. If you are someone with bruised credit, look for a lender who will take all the factors (length of time on job, length of time in current profession, current skill level at that profession, past history of steady income, etc) into consideration before they give you an answer as to whether or not to lend you money.

Let me say, all of this conversation about lending and borrowing money may make you think that I am an advocate of lots of debt. Actually, if you have the choice to owe or not owe, I would say you should pick to not owe. When you have little or no debt you are not a slave to your creditor. I believe that debt is a tool that can be used to work to your advantage. This takes understanding debt as it pertains to your life goals. If debt will get you where you want to be (a home for your family, capital to start a new business venture, etc.) then it may make good business sense to incur debt. What we must learn is the difference between good debt and bad debt.

Good debt allows someone with a good credit history, steady income and some money saved to purchase a home. If the average person were to wait until they saved up enough to buy a house, they would probably never own one. Homes can run in the $100,000 and above range and for most of us, we just don't have that kind of money sitting in an account that we can use for a home purchase. So we borrow money from a lender and invest it in an appreciating item.

Bad debt on the other hand, is usually high interest rates charged on some item that depreciates in value instead of appreciating. These types of debt can strangle you and keep you under the yoke of bondage. Examples would be 24% rates on furniture that won't last longer than the note you signed to purchase it. We must work to get out from under all bad debts as quick as possible and if we are going to have debt, let it be good debt.

We have those in the success race who just won't try. They don't even attempt to use debt, good or bad, to their advantage. They are defeated before they even begin. Since they see others faster than they are who are in the race, they say what's the use of running? When financial calamity hits these people they almost never recover. But let me ask you a question; what endeavor have you ever gotten into that has not been faced with adversity? Who has ever accomplished anything of significance that has not paid a great price to do it? If it is worthwhile, it comes with a price. And the greater the prize the greater the price.

Remember, it is not what happens to you that determines your destiny; rather it is what you allow to happen within you that matters most. This comes about by how you interpret the affairs of your life. Life can make you or break you. Everyone gets knocked down but do you have what it takes to get back up? Only you can answer that. The good news is that if you are determined to succeed, others may get in your way but only you can stop you. And this gives you the power to keep your destiny in your own hands. If someone fails, they cannot blame it on others for even though it is easier when we have help, the truth is, and you can make it without help (it just takes more time). This means that you have your destiny in your hands and that is where it belongs.

This doesn't mean that we don't need anyone. We do. Successful people rarely stand alone. But what I am saying is that success must come individually first. If all you do is wait until others come to make you the success you hope to be, you will be sadly mistaken.

Ok, you have made the assessment honestly. You know exactly where you are financially. So what do you do with this information? We need to create a plan for our freedom but there is one element you need before you get into your plan. You need faith! That is the topic of our next discussion.

Everything Starts with Faith (you've got to believe)

Mark 9:23 – All things are possible to him that believes

No matter how good a plan you come up with, if you don't believe that the plan will work, it probably won't. The fuel for any good strategy is not only that it is a good strategy but that somebody believes it has a chance to succeed.

As you progress along the path to recovery, you will have to make adjustments in your plan. You may come into some unexpected money or have some debt reduced quicker than you had anticipated. That is ok. Fine-tuning your plan along the way is not a problem as long as you end up where you originally intended, free.

Many times our circumstances blind us to possibilities. We see the income we are making and in our minds believe that it would be impossible for us to overcome our financial mountains. Or we make the mistake of thinking that it will take our whole lifetime before we come to realize the freedom we so desperately crave. Yet this is rarely the case at all. On the contrary, dreams pick up speed when they are believed in.

You may not have enough income to do what you need to have done. But with faith and a dream, you can see yourself doing something else that will affect how much money you have to work with. Maybe you need to go to school and further your education. Or maybe you are just in the wrong field. There is more than enough money in this world to meet the needs of all; you just have to learn how to attract more of it to you. A rule of thumb in this area is this: *people are prepared to pay for what they perceive benefits them. We must learn how to deliver more of what they see as benefits.*

I spent my early years in sales. Although I felt this was something I wanted to do I realized that in order to be good at it and to receive proper compensation for my efforts would require that I become well prepared. So I started to study the art of sales. I began reading books that dealt with sales and sales techniques. I started attending sales seminars to get ideas about how to be better at my craft. I listened to a variety of tapes on issues such as negotiations, understanding the sales process, sales management, etc. Anyone who wants to be good at their craft should become a student of that craft and work diligently to perfect it.

But there was another dilemma I started to encounter as I approached my late 20's. Even though I had started to prepare myself and was achieving a level of sales success (winning awards and receiving company and industry recognition) I discovered that whenever I wanted to make a move which I felt would enhance my career, my lack of a formal education got in the way. As a young man I had went to college for a while but I didn't feel that I needed a four-year education for a career in sales. After all, if I am a good communicator and understand the sales process, I should do just fine. But many companies had a bachelor's degree as one of the requirements to even warrant an interview. So I started to feel like I had this stigma to overcome.

As a Christian I was more concerned about learning about God than business. I did not feel the need or desire to pursue a business degree. I did attend a business college and complete a one-year program but that was not my desire. So I was faced with a career decision. Do I get an education just for the sake of a job or do I get an education in what I really want and learn what I need for my job.

This is where faith comes in. I went to school and completed my degree in Biblical Studies. Then I trusted that if I were to remain in the workforce as a salesman, the fact that I now had a degree (which I could make use of personally) along with experience and a track record of success (in the field that I was working in) that I now had the necessary ingredients to work for whatever sales organization I wanted to.

This changed how I looked for employment. I became very industry specific. I wanted a job in a field where I already had knowledge of the product. I had worked in real estate, insurance and mortgages, so that is where I focused my attention. Because of faith in my God, my plan and my purpose, I found that these industries were very warm and receptive to me. The degree helped to open doors for interviews and the experience allowed me to sell myself once I got in. I found my income steadily increasing and my personal financial situation getting better as I got older.

You see, someone must believe in you. Someone must have enough faith in your potential to take a chance with you. It should start with you. How can you go forward if you have trouble believing that you can? It took me years to finish my bachelors but since then I went on to complete my Masters and Doctorate degree. I had to believe in me and I needed to have someone else to do so as well.

My wife provided unlimited support to the dream of our being free financially. She encouraged me when the world was discouraging. Even when we both knew that I was being treated unfairly she would remind me that education and experience would allow me to come to doors of opportunity which could open if I had faith and believed in God.

Now I know for some, the whole idea of faith in God represents a problem. The thing to remember about faith is that it is no greater than the object to which it is directed. If you have faith in yourself that is fine but you and I are plagued with limitations. A faith in God opens a door to having one place faith in something bigger than yourself.

I have yet to find a truly successful person who enjoys life on all levels (physical, emotional, financial, social, mental, and spiritual) who does not have some type of understanding and relationship with a power greater than themselves. Unless we see how the creator fits into the grand scheme of life, we will never come to enjoy life at its fullest.

Another reason why faith is so important is that it will shorten your stay in a problem.

What took you years to get into with poor planning may take only months to get out of with the proper focus. (Now I am not advocating that we look for easy solutions). Be prepared to give as much time to coming out as you did getting into trouble. With faith it may happen in a shorter time but be prepared nevertheless. And how do you help yourself to believe that things will be different with you? How do you prepare yourself for the new future that awaits you? There are a couple of practical things we can do to build our faith as we prepare to implement our plan.

First, *what do you see*? Can you visualize yourself in a different situation? Can you see yourself with no more calls from creditors? Can you see yourself living where you want to, driving what you want and wearing what you want? I am not talking about becoming preoccupied with stuff. I am speaking of living the life that you feel you were predestined to live.

Each of us is born into a particular world and set of circumstances. In order to reach the people in your world you will need to have a certain level of success. People are not attracted to people who look like failures and act like it. You and I have a responsibility to reach the world we live in positively and that will require influence. Understanding this means that if I need to dress a certain way to impact my world, and then I want to have the resources to do so.

In the sales field image is everything. When I first got into sales I drove a beat up car that was very dependable. It was just loud. I'll never forget going on a sales call and after making the sale having the customer want to come out and walk me to my car. They were trying to see what I was driving. I played it off by saying that I had some other business to take care of in the neighborhood and would not be leaving soon. I ended up going to the corner and spending some time in the store, just waiting for the chance to sneak into my car and leave without this customer seeing me. I learned something that day; in order to be successful; I have to start looking successful. This would do 2 things; it would have people confident to do business with me and it would give me an inner confidence that I had achieved some level of success, thus not needing to be ashamed of anything I owned.

Now there are those who say that we should not pay so much attention to things like the type of car we drive. But let me ask you a question; don't you have a mental picture come into your mind everytime you hear the word Mercedes? Lexus? BMW? Pinto? Chevette? Don't misunderstand me. There is nothing wrong with any of the cars that I have just mentioned. But each carries with it a certain stigma, if you will. Whether you agree with it or not people live by association and make mental assessments based on what they currently believe. Instead of trying to tell the world they are wrong in believing as they do, we need to understand what they believe and then work the system.

Personally, cars are not my thing. I want one that looks nice, runs nice and accommodates my family size. I am not real caught up in what type it is. Of course I have my preferences like everyone else. But to me cars are just tools to get the job done. I refused to be preoccupied with them.

Whatever it is that paints a picture of success for you is what you must start seeing what you believe. It is important that you see yourself possessing what you profess. This is faith. Second, *what do you hear?* Many grow up in an environment where the adults do not realize the importance of saying the right things to children. Many adults today grew up hearing they were stupid would not amount to anything, worthless, etc. These types of negative comments only hurt the self-esteem of the child. No wonder so many today are looking to find themselves and are on a search for significance.

Years ago I taught 5th and 6th grade Sunday school at our church. On one particular Sunday I asked my group of 40 students, "What are you going to do when you are grown up"? Surprisingly, many of my students had absolutely no idea as what they would do once grown. However, one of my students replied " I haven't decided yet just what I will be when I am grow up but of this I am certain; whatever it is, I will definitely be successful."

His answer intrigued me so I asked him to explain it further. He said "My father has told me since I can remember that I am a child of destiny, born to do something great with my life. I have no choice but to expect greatness for it is what I was created to do." I used this answer as an object lesson for the children gathered there that day. How many adults would live different lives if they understood that they too have been created to fulfill a destiny? Sadly, too many of us believe that whatever hand life deals us, we are forced to have to play it.

Say it! If no one else believes in you, you must start believing in yourself. We can't wait until others begin to notice that our lives have meaning and that we have a plan to fulfill. So we must stand center stage and allow ourselves to grow into the man or woman we were created to be.

Third, *what do you believe?* As we see and say, we must believe. No matter what anyone has told you, you are special. What's more, you are the only you. This world would not be better because you are gone but is better because you are here.

Believe that you are unique. Believe that there is a place for you that you were made to fill and only you can make it happen. Believe in what you can do, where you are going and how much better people will be because you have arrived.

Somebody in this world has a need. Maybe they need an encouraging word and you are that mouthpiece. Maybe they need a hug or just a touch of acceptance and you are the hand to bring it. Maybe it's just a smile. See your worth and eternal value to life.

This book is about fixing the mess that you may find yourself in. If you can see it, say it, and believe it, you are on your way to *fixing it*.

Fourth, what can you conceive? You see it. You hear it. You believe it. Now you must make use of your imagination so that you can conceive it. Too many times greatness stops in the area of belief. But we need to go beyond seeing that something is possible and hearing that it is possible. We must move beyond believing it is possible to conceiving the impossible so that we can make it possible.

Conceiving is like giving birth. When a woman is pregnant she is said to have conceived. But what has she actually done? She has taken a fertilized seed and planted it within herself. In time with the proper nutrients and under the proper conditions the seed within her will grow from a conceived seed to a mature one. Our ideas are like that. They must be conceived. They must be planted within our own hearts and allowed to flourish. We must see ourselves the way we envision our lives to be. Everything starts with a seed and our great ideas are no exception.

Fifth, you must achieve it. It is not enough to have a belief in your mind or to conceive in your heart that what you believe is possible and will come to pass. Now you must put feet to your faith. You must take positive steps toward the realization of your plan. (In the next chapter we will be talking more in detail about the plan). There is something invigorating about accomplishing goals. Like the artist who looks back at a finished piece of art we must look back at where we were and the progress we have made since we started to have faith in a better tomorrow.

Imagine that you have been invited to a friend's house for a get together. You are very tired after working all day and yet you push yourself to go on. As you enter his house it is crowded and all you want is a chair to sit down. Now you can walk into a room full of people and see an empty chair. You hear the guest in the house say to you, "Just find you somewhere to sit". You can walk over to the chair. In your mind you may see the many times that you have watched other people sit in chairs. You believe that if they can sit down and not fall to the floor you will too. You conceive in your heart what it will be like to sit down and take a load off your feet. But until you actually achieve the goal of sitting in the chair (pulling it out from the table, getting in front of it and positioning yourself to sit down) you will never experience the rest that comes from finding a seat when you have been on your feet for a long time.

WE MUST BECOME ACHIEVERS. We must condition ourselves to having dreams, seeing those dreams fulfilled, seeing ourselves after the dream and then going after whatever we need to so that the dream will happen. We must get away from accepting and believing that mediocrity and average is to be our norm. Nothing is farther from the truth. Do you see greatness in yourself? Do you see someone who, when you look in the mirror, is a winner? If not, then you need to get yourself a new mirror. Because if all you see is failure and defeat, someone on their last leg about to be counted out of the game, then you see the wrong person. No, there is greatness inside of you and faith allows you to access that greatness and become all that you were created to be. You don't have to settle for less.

The way we cease to settle is to believe for what we know we can have. This means that we must see it. We have spoken about the fact that you must see something first. An old saying in the world is "you must see it to believe it". Yet when we understand what it means to walk by faith, we say "you must believe it to see it". *For you will never see what you are unwilling to believe.* It must exist in you before you see it manifest outside of you. There is nothing mystical or magical about it. Our lives generally end up where we expect them to be so if you want to have a better life, you must learn to expect one.

Think about self-image. The picture you have of yourself on the inside of you defines your self-image. This picture is formed early in life. If your parents told you as a child that you were stupid, slow and good for nothing, these words have helped to shape your self-image. Either you embraced and agreed with them or you went against what they said and believed something different. Many times, those who have not agreed with the limitations placed on them by others have found themselves working to prove the doubters wrong.

It is about how we see ourselves. Oh, we know that the world sees us in a particular way. But we also see ourselves. And the picture you have of you is the one that really matters. You see, *you will never rise above the level of your self-image.* If you see yourself as a failure, you will remain one, regardless of any success you might come to enjoy. But if you see yourself as a success, you will become one, regardless of what failure you may have to overcome to get there.

Imagine that growing up your father told you "if a man earns $8 an hour, he can consider himself to have arrived. There is no more to life than earning $8.00 an hour." Now maybe in the days of your father $8 an hour meant a lot but in the time and day we live in, it really doesn't. So as a young man you get a job and earn $6.75 an hour. Because you are a good worker you start to prosper on the job and see yourself getting raises. $7.00. $7.25, $7.50, $7.75 and then what? Now you are on the brink of breaking the $8.00 mark. What does that mean to you?

You remember what your father told you about $8.00. You now have a choice. If you have internalized his words and made them your own, you may believe that there is no reason to make more than $8.00 per hour for at $8.00 you will have arrived. If your job takes you past $8.00 it will mess with your preconceived ideas about success. Well, you can't have that so you make plans to (subconsciously) to make sure that you never grow beyond $8.00 an hour. You will mess up this new job if that is what it will take to keep you at this level. It is subconscious sabotage.

I saw this phenomenon occurring in the life of my father. He had a high school education and did not believe that he deserved to reach certain levels in life. Whenever the opportunity presented itself for him to grow, he would turn it down so that he could stay in that safe, secure, set environment. Now only was he afraid to succeed, he was afraid to go beyond where he had been. And he gladly received the limitations placed on him by others. But he was a talented man. His only drawback is that he did not understand this principle of limitation

That is why faith is so important if we are ever going to break the cycle of mediocrity. You will never rise above the mental picture you have of yourself. That is why we must expose ourselves to the greater things in life. I am not saying that everyone will be rich or that we should covet to have lots of things. What I am saying is that it is natural to want to do better tomorrow than you are doing today. To settle for the comforts that you may enjoy now when there is so much more is to shortchange yourself.

I have been blessed to visit many of the cities of our nation. Although I live in Chicago, it never ceases to amaze me of the many beauties that exist elsewhere. If all I did was say that Chicago is ok with me, it is what I am use to and I want to see nothing else (which by the way, was the way I use to think) then I would have missed out. There are a lot of interesting cities and places to visit. We should not limit ourselves to just what we are use to.

Let me say that I believe I have the cure for small thinking. It is EXPOSURE. We must expose ourselves to what this life has to offer. We must expose ourselves to people who are doing better in certain areas than we are. We must begin to see that there are those who are not limited by small thinking and refuse to allow themselves to become contaminated with the seeds of failure. Many a times a successful person will not even associate with someone who is an obvious failure for they don't want that defeatist attitude to rub off on them.

We must open up our minds to the realm of possibility. When we seek to see what is and what can be, the possibilities become endless. There is so much more to life than what any of us can see. There is the blessing of having a good family, people whom you love and who love you. A great job where you enjoy getting up and going to work every day. I must admit, I have not had much of that in my life for my jobs have been just that, a job.

Let me say this. I can look back over my life and see times where the people who were over me purposely did things to limit me. Sometimes it was their intention. Other times I think it was just ignorance (they did not know how to help subordinates achieve their goals) or intimidation (it takes a secure leader to work with another secure leader who is subordinate to them and not abuse their position).Whatever the case was, I always made it my case to remain focused on the goals that had been set within me. There were stages in my life that I wanted to reach by a certain time. I refused then and I still refuse today to be limited by another man's lack of vision. Listen, if you ever desire to do anything great with your life, then you must refuse to let people define you. In their definition of where you should be and where you should live and how much you should earn, you will discover that it is typically not where you could be if you only believed.

LIFE WITHOUT LIMITS! Strive to live in such a way that you and only you, set the limits by which you will live by. Don't let anyone, including yourself, deny you of the future that has been laid out for you. You are the result of a divine intention and there is a place for you to occupy here on earth. It has your name on it. Your space has already been carved out in the land of destiny. Believe and you will conceive. Therefore, go for it!

What is Your Plan

Proverbs 16:9 – A man's heart devises his way

The assessment of your current situation has been made. You understand the place that faith has in making your way to the top financially. And now you are faced with this question; what is my plan? How do I get to where it is I know I want to go?

Plans are like roadmaps. They allow you to travel from your destination of not being in the place of your dreams to the place that you have always dreamed of. When we think of taking a vacation and traveling across the country, it is unwise to do so without a plan. How long do we estimate it will take us to get there? What provisions do we need to carry to make our trip successful? Should we drive, take the bus or fly by plane? Decisions, decisions, so many decisions.

Sad to say, most people spend more time planning their next vacation than they have planning the course of their life. The average person does not even know where they hope to be next year because, for many of us, living by expectation is foreign. Instead of approaching life to see what we can make happen, we just let life happen to us. This can make you a victim of circumstances instead of a victor over them.

Speak your vision! It is very hard to rise above any situation that you are afraid to speak of. If you cannot form your lips to say *"debt free"*, how will you see it realized in your life? It is very hard to rise above the level of your confession. This does not mean that you go around and say 'I am rich, I am rich", expecting just this phrase to cause riches to come to you. That in and of itself does not change anything. It is the belief in oneself and the plan's ability to succeed that causes the plan to prosper.

See your vision! The question that must be asked often is "what do you see?" Can you see yourself without those bill collectors calling? Can you see the day when you won't have to count every penny because there will be some money left over? Will you ever be able to go on vacation and not have to worry about how to pay for it? Can you live without using credit to make ends meet?

Write down the vision (plan). Make it plain; make it so that others who see it may run with it. To get where you want to go will require the help of others. Anyone who thinks they are successful without the help of others needs to think again. In order to get where we want to go, someone must be there for us. Someone must purchase your product or service. Someone must give you an opportunity. Someone must believe in you. When the people who believe in us see where we want to go, it creates a wave that our vision is able to ride upon.

My wife's greatest asset to me is her ability to believe in me. Whenever I have gone to her with an idea (and some of them have been pretty far fetched), I have found her to be very supportive. Now, she doesn't throw good sense out the window as she expresses her faith in me. She will ask me the hard questions and help me to think through what I want to do.

But she never belittles me for dreaming or puts me down. She makes me feel like my dream is important and I am just the man to do it. She has faith in me. I cannot tell you how many times this has been just the boost I need, to have someone believe in me and show concern for how I turn out.

Find someone you can share your dreams with. When we first wanted to buy our house, people whom we know and loved told us we were too young to be homeowners. My own parents tried to dissuade me. But my wife told me that she believed we could do it and it really didn't matter if anyone understood. It was to be our house and our responsibility. So I went forth with full force and I am so glad I did.

Plans have a way of taking a life of their own. It is amazing the power we are able to unleash when we know where we are going. In my late teens I took a job working with a clothing manufacturer. My job description was a billing clerk. After being there a couple of months I decided that I wanted to work to move up in the company. I understood that in order to be promoted, I would need to increase my value to the organization.

I created a plan. First, I survey my present surrounding and decided what area of this company I wanted to work in. Now, there were many places I could work but very few that would be suited to my own gifts and abilities. I saw that I wanted to work in the accounting office because I was good with numbers and wanted to learn more things about money.

But I saw a number of obstacles to getting into this office. First, I didn't have any formal accounting training. Although I was in college my major was science because I wanted to do research. So I checked out what starting research assistants would make at that time (which was about $15,000 at the time) and I decided that I didn't want to go to school for 4 years to earn $15,000. So I switched and started taking business classes, particularly accounting. I learned enough to qualify for an entry-level bookkeeping position at my company in about a year.

Second, they had never had a male in that position before. In my life I have felt the brunt of not being able to do because of something that is entirely out of your control (age, race, etc). Since I knew that I would never stop being a man (and I didn't want to, either), I had to see how to address that issue with my boss when it came up.

Third, I understood that in order to be promoted, I must be promotable. This would mean that I had to outgrow my present position. So that is what I did. I asked my boss how many orders a day the biller before me had processed. He said, oh it was anywhere between 6-8 an hour. If the biller ever hit 10, it was a miracle". Then I asked, what would be an optimum production requirement for a biller and he said "as many as possible but if we could get 8-9 an hour done, it would be great". So I now knew what my predecessor did and how much they would like to see. At that time I was doing about 6 – 7 an hour so I wasn't setting any records. But I also knew that I was intentionally slow. Math was one of my better subjects and if I used what I already had I could better my present situation. I arranged the orders so that the easy ones were first. I took all the orders that were small and would not require me to use a calculator. These I knew I could process and give to the shipping clerk. When I stopped taking the orders back to my desk and using the calculator it saved me minutes on each order. So I hurried up on these small orders and gave the shipping clerk something to do. To my surprise maybe 60-65% of the orders for the day I could do in my head. So in about an hour's time, I had enough work done to keep the shipper busy till late afternoon (we started early in the morning).

Then I took the orders that needed a calculator and put them in order from smallest to the largest. The reason I left the largest for last was although it would take me longer to process them, the shipping clerk would spend almost the same amount of time on larger orders as he did on small ones. So I gave him a backlog of orders that would give me time to work on the larger ones without him waiting around for me to finish. I then would spend the majority of my day working on the more complicated orders. By 2:00 pm everyday I was done with my work for the day and started planning the next days work. When I got ahead of the factory to the point where there were no more orders I went to help the shipper (although I never wanted to make him look bad so I turned it into a learning experience and in time I could perform his job as well).

Soon my boss came over wanting to know my secret. Since it took someone good in math to do it the way I was doing it they understood that no one could just come in off the street and use my system and succeed as I did. Eventually they allowed me to finish my work and then spend some time in the bookkeeping office, helping out where I could.

I learned how our systems functioned internally and I learned something about being in business that was to help me in years to come. There were some who got mad at me and said I was making them look bad. But my focus was on my plan. I wanted to be so good in my current position that I could be promoted to another one. Some became intimidated by my desire to learn and the way I used my gifts to make room for me. When you realize that you happen to be good at something, don't let the fact that other people are not good at it intimidate you. If anything, they need to find out what they are good at and give it their all.

You see when it come to making a plan work there are three things to keep in mind; *use what you have, where you are, when you can*. To make any plan work requires understanding what resources are available to you so that you can bring them to bear on your situation. The writing of this book is the result of a plan.

I learned that there are three things that I am to focus my attention on. (Remember, this is the plan for my life. Your plan is different and will require things from you that my plan did not require of me and vice versa.) Until you know what you are called to do, you will most likely spend your life trying to be someone else instead of being the person you were created to be.

First, I discovered that I am to be in full time ministry. I have a real heart for meeting the real, relevant needs in people. This type of work fitted well with my gifts and interests. As such I have devoted myself to becoming the very best minister I can be.

Second, I have a passion for writing. I believe this comes from my love of reading. I have grown so much through books and other materials. I want to give back in printed form to others out there who are like me. So I studied writing to discover just what makes a good writer great. I am still a student and will be for years to come.

Third, I wanted to own my own business. I am not a believer in the America dream of "your future lies in corporate America". Given the downturn and instability of most jobs, I don't think it wise to depend strictly on a job where you work for someone else. America was built on the concept of free enterprise and many people with good ideas turned them into great opportunities that have helped millions.

It is possible to have a good job and to enjoy it. We need to strive for that. But to trust that someone else will take care of your future is not how I see life as being lived. When we take our own future into our hands, we cease to blame others when things don't turn out right.

I sold Real Estate for 9 years on both a full and part time basis. During that time I became a Real Estate Broker and spent 2 years in management so this gave me a good understanding of how the business worked. It also gave me an idea of what it would be like being in business for myself. There are some benefits to self-employment but it's not all a bed of roses.

There are two types of income a person can earn. The first is *active income,* where you are doing something everyday to create the income you receive. When we receive an hourly wage, we are receiving active income. *Passive income* is what we receive as a result of work we have already done. The royalties a musician receives from a CD sale is an example of passive income. It's also called residual income.

If we are looking to improve our financial condition (and many problems we have are financially connected), then increasing the amount of passive income we receive can help us to achieve our goals. Too many people base their financial future on active income.

Everyone needs a plan. A wise man learns by listening. Let me share with you some nuggets that have helped me as I have worked to become debt free. Now I am not at the place I want to be, but I understand that every journey begins with a single step.

1) If creditors are on your back, pay attention. The worst thing you can do to someone you owe money to is ignore them (been there, done that). Instead, contact your creditors and make arrangements based on what your current situation is. If you really have no money to send to them, tell them. Just remember, they don't want to hear that you will not be paying them. Since you do owe them, give them a time when they can expect to receive some money from you. And whenever it is possible, send more than you agreed.

Remember, your creditor does not live with you. Don't allow someone who is not a part of your household to dictate what you will do. It makes no sense for your family to starve while you are paying off your bills. Yes, you do owe them but you owe it to yourself to live. So cut back even if it may not be possible to cut some things completely off.

2) Whenever you do pay something off, CELEBRATE! You may not be able to go out and spend a lot of money but you can go out and just appreciate the fact that your hard work has paid off. To get to where you want to go it will take a few victories under your belt. So celebrate each one.

3) Remind yourself that where you are today is not where you will be tomorrow. If you really don't like your present situation, refuse to see it as your final situation. It is possible to be crying today and smiling tomorrow.

In order for your plan to be a good plan, it will need some necessary components inside of it to make it realistic. Some of those things are;

1) *It must be written down.* To have this plan just in your head will make it hard for you to stay focused. You must see it written down plainly where you can refer to it often.
2) *It must be understandable.* How can you follow a plan that you don't understand? If it makes sense to no one else, it must make sense to you.
3) *It must have a clear start date.* The best-made plans are just that unless they have a time when all the ideas are to be put into motion. When you have examined your options and put together your plan, know when you will be starting it.
4) *It should have an estimated ending time.* This is important. If your plan is to go on from here to eternity it will be very hard to stay focused. Every tunnel has light at the end of it or it is just a dead end. Even if you do not make your ending goal, at least you have something to aim for. Most plans may take a couple of years to complete and if so, we should plan to be involved for the long haul.
5) *It must be realistic.* If you earn $30,000 a year and say that within six months you will have $100,000 saved strictly from your salary it may be possible but is highly

unlikely. Your plan must make sense. It must have realistic expectations. Don't expect to do in a short time what it took you a long time to mess up. A good rule of thumb is to give yourself as much time coming out of debt as it took you to get into it. Remember to be anxious for nothing.

6) *It must be simplistic.* Easy to understand. Hopefully, real easy. This means that you should be able to follow your plan without a lot of additional calculations once you have put the plan in place. It should flow smoothly.

7) *You should create it and then revise it.* It is very hard to come up with something that after one try is perfect. Many times you will create a rough draft that captures your main intentions and then come back and fine-tune it for details.

8) *Revisit it after a month.* When it has been in place for at least a month, sit down and revisit the entire plan. Look at what is working and see how you can improve upon it. Look at what is not working and see how you can change it.

9) *Remember what makes this a good plan in the first place; it's your plan.* You put this together (maybe with the help of others) but it is still your plan. So take ownership and be glad that you have your own plan.

10) *After your plan has accomplished your goal, don't neglect creating plans for future goals.* Getting debt free is just a stop on the journey of life. You will not have arrived just because you don't owe anyone. Instead, set higher goals that you can reach for and continue to grow so that you will not become stagnant in the process.

You must stay focused as you work your plan. There will be some well meaning but ignorant people who will get in the way. Now I am not talking about those who intentionally try to make you fail (and you may have a few of those). No, I am speaking of those who have good intentions but get in your way. They are the ones who say things like "it can't be done. No one has done that before. And what makes you think that you can do this?"

I find it very difficult to discuss my dreams with people. Throughout the years people have tried to discourage me by reminding me of my limitation. So what I would end up doing is coming up with a plan and just working it. When I get to the other side and the dream has become a reality, then people would get with the program. But by that time, it was too late for me.

I use to tell my wife when we were dating "Stick with me and I will set you free. Free from the limitations that currently bind you and keep you down. I have a dream and I am going somewhere. Where that is I don't know but if you stay with me, you will get to enjoy it when we get there. You see, when I am on the top I won't need you. It's on the way up that is so hard."

My wife has given to me the greatest gift a man can get from a partner; she believes in me and in my dreams. If I were to tell her "honey, I believe that I am to go and purchase the Sears Tower in downtown Chicago, she would say, if you believe it, go for it. I am with you." I have told her often it is her belief in me that keeps me going when I want to quit. And that is why every one of us needs someone who will believe in us. Someone who has faith in our potential. I believe that someone is so important to your future success. If at all possible, you above all other people should believe in you. But if you don't then you will need someone else who will. This can help you to start to believe in yourself.

Maybe it will be a teacher who says you are not dumb or unable to learn. Maybe it's a parent who is willing to show the world that their child has what it takes to make an impact in this society. Maybe it's a good friend who sees what you could be but loves you as you are. Whoever it may be, they will have to have eyes that see your potential.

This is why we need a plan. We need a roadmap. And there may be those who don't help you to develop the plan but believe that you can achieve it. So they support and encourage you along the way. No one ever experiences true, lasting success alone. We all need somebody to believe in us and help us.

Plans provide purpose. They not only give us a way to see where we are going, they give us a reason for taking the trip. Let's assume you are in the process of purchasing your first home. Before you ever start looking at homes, you first need to come up with a plan or strategy to acquire it. You assess what you will need and from who. You know you don't have the money to pay cash so you will need a bank. You don't know where the houses for sale are, so you use a realtor. In addition you might get an attorney and a home inspector to assist you.

Since you know nothing about the lending process you feel in the dark as you step out to accomplish this goal. You go to a bank and find out that you can qualify for a loan of $150,000. You decide that the house you will eventually purchase needs 3 bedrooms and 2 baths. You get with a realtor who shows you 4 houses and decide to purchase one. You put in a contract, close on your financing and take possession of the home. (By the way, the process is almost never this easy).

A wise person does not go out and begin to do. They sit down and consider the cost involved. They plan. They strategize. They prepare. There is nothing wrong with being prepared for if you were doing this right, you should be able to see where you are going long before you got there.

Plans give us vision. They help to see farther with clearer vision. This is especially true when we consider fixing financial struggles. If you hope to get to the place of true financial freedom, it will require embracing a plan and then sticking to it. Since the plan provides the roadmap, we can rely on it to take us to our anticipated destination. And that plan must include the understanding of how credit is.

Understanding and Making Use of Credit

Romans 13:8 – Owe no man anything, except to love him

We live in a society where everything seems to be going up. Houses in good neighborhoods can run in the hundred of thousands of dollars. Cars for twenty to thirty thousand dollars are not uncommon. Banks have more fees than ever before, food is not getting any cheaper and it is costing more to live daily.

On the other side there are those who are working and yet their salary does not keep pace with inflation. Even with an inflation rate of 3% (a modest estimation) it would take only a few years before one becomes aware that what they earn is not enough. For most families they are trapped working a job with limited increases and facing the stress of watching the cost of living growing outside their reach. That is one of the reasons why we see so many adults returning to school, in the hopes of making things better for themselves and to open doors for promotion.

In light of this, what is the obvious solution for the typical American? *Credit!*

For many, this is the way to offset the lack of income necessary to live. Very few people can afford to own a home upright but the use of credit will allow someone to purchase a home typically with little or even no money down. Good credit allows you to purchase a brand new car, new furniture, etc. many times with no money. Credit can be used to purchase groceries, fuel, household items and many of the desires of the average person. It can for the most part take the place of cash and if one is not careful it will fool you into believing that you actually have lots of money.

In essence credit does not necessarily mean you have lots of money, you only have lots of potential. Credit is making use of someone else's resources to purchase items that are desired. In and of itself this is not bad. However it does raise some questions.

There appears to be a paradox in place. Credit is good in that without it, most Americans would live at a level far below what they have become accustomed to. Those who extend credit know this and make calculated attempts to use credit to allow people to have what they otherwise could not afford. The question with credit use is not "how much does this cost me" but "what will be my monthly payments." If the payments are affordable typically it is a smart purchase (or so we have been told).

In the Old Testament there was a principle called the Jubilee. It was not uncommon for people to come into some type of slavery to either pay off a debt or as a result of being conquered. Yet most debts that were incurred by the Lord's chosen people Israel were designed to end within a seven-year period. After the seven years were up the servant was given the option to go free. In addition they were not sent away empty-handed but with some goods in their possession to give them a head start in their new life.

Once every 50 years was known as the year of Jubilee, where everyone's property reverted back to its original owner and the people who were in debt were made free. God understood that debt was a weight and must be relieved at some point in a person's life. Proverbs 22:7 say "the *rich rule over the poor and the borrower is servant to the lender.*"

Today people who get into credit can have loans that last for 30 years. The problem with this is the length of term. Years ago mortgage loans with little or no money down were unheard of. People were given the opportunity to own provided they had money for a down payment. They also were given a few years to make the payments. Now the longer amortization and the lower down payments have allowed untold millions to purchase property but at an awesome price.

Credit is a wonderful tool. It is almost impossible to travel without large sums of money if you have no credit. You need a credit card to rent a car, a hotel room and to make reservations over the phone. If one is in business it becomes a hindrance to progress if a check or cash must accompany every decision you make to purchase. Whether it is in business or for personal use, there are those who don't use it at all and although there is some wisdom to that decision, I believe it is better to understand how to control credit than to stop using it altogether.

I have the distinct advantage of being someone who has had bad credit (and felt the curse of what it is to live with that in today's society) and to have good credit. It is important as an individual that you protect your right to have good credit. It is one thing if you are able to purchase something and make use of credit yet you chose not to. That is you right and your prerogative. But it is another thing to have bad credit, want to use credit and to be told that you cannot.

From the time that I was 19 years old until I was married with children I had what you would consider bad credit. I purchased a car from a finance company with an interest rate of over 30 %. My original purchase price for the car was $1495. I put down about $150 to just cover plates and some of the administrative costs of purchasing. My payments were $60 /month for what I thought was to be about 3 years. After almost 3 years of making this $60 payment I found myself caught with about $3000 in bills. As a young man with creditors calling me day and night, I didn't know what to do. The advice I got haunted me for years to come.

You see many people who don't understand credit and finances will give you very strange advice. For example, some told me "aw, don't worry about it. Don't pay your bills. What can they do to you anyway?" That advice can cost you big.

Then there were others who said "no matter what, pay your bills". So I could have nothing to eat for 3 days but as long as my bills were paid, I was doing the right thing.

Through it all, I learned a painful lesson; it really does not matter what you pay for an item, what matters most is how you structure the purchase. If someone offers you a house for $350,000 and today it is only worth $150,000, most people would say that it would be foolish to purchase that house. Yet if the owner gave you a monthly note of $100 and said that the payments would stay at $100 for the next 40 years with no hope of going up you might consider. In addition if they were to take that $350,000 note and secure it by your name only instead of making it collateral for the house, you might think even harder. What is they also said that the loan was due only as long as you were alive but the minute you died the loan died with you and was not held against your estate, what would you say? This is a ridiculous loan but it serves to prove a point; under the right circumstances, even a bad deal can start to look good.

The car loan looked good to me initially. It was with a low down payment and low monthly payments. What I had not paid attention to was the interest rate and how long it would have taken me to pay it off. When I look back I realized that I was taken for a ride. This loan would have become a nightmare unless I came up with a way to pay it off. I did eventually get it paid off but I paid much more for this car than I should have.

When you have this type of credit profile (slow pays on previous credit purchases), it becomes very difficult to get unsecured credit. This is the type of credit that does not ask for collateral in return. So credit cards were out for me. In addition now I was considered a high risk so even when I went after secured credit items (such as a house and car) I paid a very high interest rate. When a person falls behind on their mortgage it is not uncommon for them to fall behind on all of their other obligations as well. It is usually very hard to get a lender to take a chance on you. When you do find one they typically offer a very high interest rate to offset the amount of risk that this loan will have. So the person with bad credit is at a double risk; not only do they pay more by way of interest than someone who has good credit, they have less money to work with because in a lot of cases if they had the money they would not have been late on their bills anyway.

I found myself as a young man already with blemished credit. It was impossible for me to get unsecured credit and so every time I went to purchase something I had to have cash. That became a real inconvenience. But I learned how to function in spite of it.

When we purchased our first house, we did what most young eager to be homeowners did; we saved money. We planned. Yet I found that the bank was reluctant to grant us our loan approval and for the life of me, I couldn't figure out why.

I finally decided to find out what the holdup was. In speaking with the mortgage lender who was doing the loan I discovered that they were really dragging their feet because of my history of slow payments. Even though I had paid off my past bad bills a few years ago, my past was creeping up to haunt me. Bad credit will do that to you; it finds you when you are sleeping. It knows when you are awake. It knows when you have been bad or good, so be good (have good credit) for goodness' sake.

Some jobs actually ran a credit report before they hired you. Since I was working in the financial arena at the time, there were some jobs I should have gotten but I could not because of my credit report. I wanted to work for a bank and that wasn't happening. So I ended up in more sales jobs, many of which were just like the peanuts an elephant gets for working in the circus.

Once we were in the house, everything I tried to buy was a hassle. I either could not qualify for it or the interest rates I paid were outrageous. It was not uncommon for me to pay 24% for 5 years for a car that barely started. Banks at that time were not too keen on opening accounts for people with bad credit so I had to search hard to find one that didn't scrutinize a lot. I wanted credit cards because I was always purchasing with cash but I had messed up the credit cards I had as a young man so I found that many credit card lenders will not give an obvious credit risk (me) more unsecured credit.

What I had in my favor was my wife. She didn't have bad credit and started working and soon our combined income was starting to look good. But I made a fatal mistake which took me years to learn and longer to correct. We made every credit application jointly and I found that now both of us were getting rejected. I wanted us to do things together, not realizing that my credit was dragging her down with me.

I didn't have a lot of credit but I had a house and then I did the next step in my pursuit of the American dream; I purchased a new car. Payments were $300/month for 60 months and since we were both working, we could afford it. Man, I was starting to feel like I was making it. I had a home, a brand new car, a job and I was only 25 years old. Some of my friends started envying me. Even my father's friends would ask me, how did you get so much stuff? You are so young! What I didn't realize is that they were right. For you see, I was in the accumulation mode as far as stuff was concerned, but I didn't have financial wisdom. We weren't saving any money and living from paycheck to paycheck. We ate out 3 or 4 times a week. We both loved to shop and buy new clothes. I was in sales and needed to purchase new suits so that I could have the right appearance.

Let me say, there is nothing wrong with wanting to enjoy this life. But the lesson my father's friends were trying to teach me is that all things come with a price. They were much older than me and had what I had but they had learned some things along the way. Me, I was in too big of a rush to see that so I just continued to keep up with the Joneses. But no one told me that they were not all they appeared to be. Theses Joneses (or Smiths or Barry's or whoever you trying to keep up with) never told anyone that all that stuff they had is not theirs and they owe their life to the creditors.

Because of my lack of foresight I did not plan for the unexpected. My wife became pregnant. And now since I had been in sales for a few years, I felt that she could stay home, raise our child and I would provide. My wife's income represented 40% of our total household budget and I guess I felt this money would just drop out of the sky when we needed it. Honestly, it did not dawn on me the financial implications her decision to stay home would have on us.

I attended a financial seminar that our church was having that year. I had a friend who was an executive with a major shoe manufacturer who happened to have 6 children at home. During the break he told me two things that I have not forgotten. He said, "Jeff, the people who need to come to these types of seminars very seldom do. If people would deal with their finances before they had a problem, they would not need so much help trying to fix them later. It's good to see you here before you have any serious financial problems." I thought to myself, boy, if he only knew what the last couple of years have been like for me.

Then he asked me how many months pregnant was my wife. I told him seven months. He said "since I see you are about to start your family, let me give you a piece of advice. When my wife and I started having children I resolved to never live off of our combined incomes. You never know how many children you will have or if, once she starts having children, she will want to continue working. Learn to live off what you make. Then she will not be forced to work when the kids come. Otherwise, the two of you will probably fight about money and your financial situation will remove her choice of being able to stay home with the children. She will have to work."

I thought about his first comment. Since that time I have determined for myself to learn about money and money management. I don't want to have financial problems and although there may be periods in my life where it will get rough, I don't want to compound it by being ignorant of what I should be doing. Financial wisdom is the key especially if you are on a tight budget.

The second suggestion hit me like a ton of bricks. We had just purchased our new car a few months earlier. Now I had a $300 car payment, $80 car insurance and a mortgage payment. We had little saved and did indeed need her income to make ends meet. After the meeting I had a heart to heart talk with my wife and we came to an understanding that proved to be very costly; in order for her to stay at home with our child, we would probably go through some rough times to make it happen.

Now don't misunderstand me. I have plenty of friends who are very career minded and good at what they do. This does not take away from them being mothers for they love their families. I don't believe it is wrong for moms to work outside the home but there could be a problem if both husband and wife focus so much on work that the family and children suffer. One of the things I have seen with my wife staying home is that she doesn't have to deal with a boss over her. She doesn't put up with irate customers. She doesn't have production deadlines or to deal with traveling far to get to work (during this time her job was about 20 miles from our house. In the winter and rush hour traffic, it would take at least an hour for her to get to work and an hour to come home). We only had one car so this put added pressure on us.

My wife needed to have a choice. Financial bondage is when you are stuck on a job and you have to take whatever they deal to you because after all, you need the money. If as a family we could live off my income, she would be free to return to work if she wanted to or to stay home with the child. I wanted so much to provide her with that choice and yet because of poor planning, I did not.

My son was born in 1988. My wife quit working and I proceeded to work harder to make up the difference. What I found is although I tried, I could not. Slowly but surely I started to fall behind. Mainly it was the car payment. But in 1989 my whole world started caving in. My mortgage payments started being late.

I looked for other work. I started working different jobs, knowing I needed a steady paycheck and benefits for my children. In Jan 1990 I finally landed what appeared to be a good job with a major insurance company. There was a steady salary and benefits. The only catch was that since it was sales, it only gave us 12 months to develop our business before it would become straight commission. But I felt that if I worked hard, with my sales background and experience, I would be able to replace the lost salary with earned commissions. I was wrong.

There is a principle to budgeting that helps you to stay within the budget. You must have an idea of how much money you will be earning and how often. When you have $100 this week, $1000 the next and $0 for the next 4 weeks, it plays havoc with your budget. It takes regularity to get out of debt. Regular received income, regular payments on your debts and regular review of your debt elimination plan to make any adjustments necessary.

I worked hard. But in 1991 my whole pay and commission structure changed. My check dropped to $3 a week. It was impossible for me to make my payments now. In addition my wife was pregnant with our second child and I couldn't just quit because I needed to have hospitalization insurance. So as my boss made my job almost impossible for me to work (he moved my desk to within inches of the woman's bathroom, gave me a desk ½ the size of the one I had before and no credenza or storage space. I guess he didn't like me much anymore since I wasn't earning him the big commissions). I understood that I need to make some extra money which I did by selling real estate on the side.

I cannot tell you the emotional, physical and mental stress I was under. All the while we were in financial straits, my wife kept getting pregnant. I had children born in 1991, 1992, 1994, 1995 and 1997. This means that all the while I was struggling with how to correct my financial situation; I was watching my family expand with growing obligations. Many said "the reason you are having so many financial struggles is that you keep having children". I knew that the reason we were having struggles was my inability to generate regular income. I was not able to consistently generate enough money to meet our obligations.

My Credit Repair Strategy

Since this chapter speaks of how to both understand and use credit, I wanted to include this section on what I did personally to reestablish myself. Now everyone has a different situation but I think you can agree with me that during this time of my life, my credit had to be pretty bad, and it was. But in just a few years, I had credit good enough to make purchases without a co signor and I believe once you understand what I came to understand, the same thing can happen to you if you so desire.

First, I had to have a personal knowledge of how credit works. I worked for a few years in the mortgage banking field and the fact that I helped a lot of people to get in homes helped me to learn about credit and how an underwriter thinks as they decide upon approving a loan for someone. When making a decision to extend credit a lender is not just looking at how much income you have but how giving you this proposed loan will affect your income in the future. Most use a ratio of some type (for example, if you earn $1000 a month and your bills with the new loan will be $900, they probably will not lend you the money). Sufficient income to cover or service the debt is necessary to borrow money.

Lenders also look at how much debt you have. They do not want you to become overextended (put into a position where you cannot pay what you owe). They look at the type of debt you have. Is it all from high interest rate finance companies? Is it all for highly consumable items or is it for items that may last you a couple of years?

What kind of work do you do? A factory worker earning $7.00/ hour driving a new car with a $550 a month note will need to show how they can afford to drive this car for it seems beyond what their current level of living can support. On the other hand, you could take this same car and give it to a mid level executive who earns $60,000 year and it will be much more agreeable to an underwriter.

Now since my credit had been damaged I understood that there were certain things I was going to have to go through that people with good credit don't. First, I would have to get use to rejection. I applied to many places for credit and got turned down. This was not to have all of these credit inquiries on my report but I knew that I would have to keep trying if I was going to find somebody willing to take a chance with me. So I applied and applied and applied.

Second, when I did get credit initially, it came at a great price. When I finally got to refinance my home I did it with an interest rate that was around 16% on an adjustable mortgage. Now this is an outrageous rate. But the lenders who work in this market understand that the people here do not have many choices and so they stuck it to me. Every six months or so I was trying to refinance so that I could get a lower rate. The catch 22 of all this is that I was already in a precarious state due to my past credit woes.

Third, I looked for ways to increase my income. I went back to school to upgrade my skills so that I could get a better paying job. The more money I had coming in, the better credit risk I would be. Lenders tend to look a little different at people who earn $40,000 a year as opposed to those who earn $12,000.

Fourth, I saved a few hundred dollars and started applying for secured credit cards. These are credit cards that if you will open up a savings account with the bank and leave the money there as collateral, they will give you a card with a credit limit equal to your deposit. The first card I got was for a $300 credit limit. I cannot tell you how I felt to once again have a credit card in my pocket. Now $300 was not a lot of money but I felt I couldn't get into too much trouble with that small a credit limit. The other advantage to this type of card is that I could always cancel it and my security deposit would cover my outstanding indebtedness so that I knew if I got rid of the card, I would leave owing the bank nothing. I also applied for some gasoline credit cards and I did get one.

Fifth, I made sure that I used each card and made more than the minimum required payment on time. I cannot stress to you how important this is to building a good credit history. Some lenders already know they are taking a risk with you when your credit has been bruised in the past. When you send in timely payments, it only strengthens your position. What you have to do is create a history of on time payments. Lenders like to see that.

Sixth, after anywhere from 6 to 12 months of making payments on time, I went to each creditor and asked for a credit line increase. The reason for this is that I wanted to see if they were the type of creditor that rewarded those who were good customers. When you deal with creditors who are use to having people with bad credit, sometimes the tendency is to believe that these people deserve their credit rating and the creditor feels they are doing you a favor by extending credit to you. Now maybe I had bad credit in the past but I was still a responsible person who was a good credit risk. So I refused to be categorized as a deadbeat. And whenever I found a creditor who would not reward those who made payments on time, I closed out the account and paid them off.

Some said I needed to make my payments longer before they could extend more credit to me. But there were some who started giving me credit, many times unsecured. The amounts were small but that was irrelevant to me. Now I started to have credit cards in my pocket that has some unsecured credit lines attached to them.

In time (1 ½ to 2 years down the road) I started applying for unsecured credit. Now I had a lot of rejections but that is ok. Eventually I got some department store cards and then I ended up with a visa card as well. I got those debit cards with my checking accounts that also serve as a credit card (you just need the money in the bank at the time of purchase). In just over 2 years I had secured credit cards, unsecured credit cards and bank debit cards. Remember, this is a process and it will take time to develop a good credit history.

There are basically three credit depositories that record the credit history of the people in this country. Each depository (Transunion, Experian and Equifax) keeps its own set of records and there may be things on your report that will show up on some but not all of the depositories. I suggest that you review your credit report from all three depositories at least once a year. You can get the information as to where they are located from the Internet with a name search. Also, anytime you apply for credit and are rejected, you should get a letter from the declining company that has the bureau that they used in part to make their decision. The mailing information is located on this rejection letter. Contact the bureau and they will send you a copy of your credit report for free. This will allow you to see just what's on your report that caused the lender to reject you.

Now let me take a moment to explain something. Depending on who you are reading regarding the subject of credit, you will find opposing viewpoints. There are those who believe that we should stay away from credit cards. They have become a snare for our society and should be avoided at all costs. There are those who have no problem with credit and believe in being heavily leveraged so that you can buy all that you can. I am not here to dispute or discuss anyone else's opinion but to share with you my own. You can do with it what you want.

I believe that credit, like money, is meant to serve us. We are not to become a slave to our possessions or our creditors. We need to have the freedom to live and use credit wisely, under supervision. If you cannot handle having a credit card in your pocket, if everytime you pass by a store the card in your pocket calls out your name, then maybe you don't need a credit card. But if you can have a card with a $5,000 or $10,000 credit limit and not spend unless it is a wise decision, then credit becomes a wonderful servant.

It allows you to keep your money in an interest earning vehicles while you use someone else's money for 30 days. This means that you get what you want, when you want it and earn interest on your money until it is time to pay for it. It allows you to make large purchases so that if you have steady income and good credit, you are able to make use of other peoples money. It allows you to have access to another safety net in case of an emergency. If something tragic happens and you needed $1,000, credit allows you to have access without using cash.

Plus, most lenders like to see someone who has used credit in the past so that they can see what type of payment history the borrower has already established. Some people believe it is best to pay cash for everything and so if you ever have to buy on credit, you will appear to be a great risk to the lender because you have paid cash for everything you needed and have no history of repayment. This doesn't make you a better risk but an unsure risk. If we want to use credit for our benefit, we need to understand it from a lenders perspective. After all, they are the ones with the money.

There are some pitfalls to avoid when building up your credit history. You want to beware of having too much credit. Don't get credit strictly for investing. Get credit that you will need. If XYZ offers a card that you can get but you know you will never shop in that store, why bother with the card? Get what you can use, not just another card to have.

You want to watch applying for too many new accounts too fast. Inquires on your report for credit will show up and be a red flag for lenders. They will want to know why you are making so many inquiries. The better way is to allow some time between inquires. Remember that you are building a credit history and histories take time. You can't rush to create a file that was not in existence yesterday.

Never, ever, ever co- sign for someone else. This means that they will use your income and credit to qualify an otherwise unqualified buyer (now this might hurt you to hear but if the bank thought they were creditworthy, they wouldn't need you to co sign). Since banks lend more money than we do it would be wise to consider their reason for requesting a co signor.

The problem here is that if you cosign for someone else, it will show up on your report as if you brought the item. Not only does that count against you for the debt, when you get ready to buy something for yourself, you are hampered. Let's say you want a house 3 years after cosigning for a loan for a relative. When you apply the bank sees this debt and you say, "I just cosigned, they pay the bill". It won't matter for you still are legally obligated for the debt.

If you just can't agree with this whole thinking on co signing, let me offer some suggestions to lesson the shock should you ever decide to cosign;

1) *Only cosign for things you can afford to pay.* What if they suddenly become unable to make the payments? Do you want to make them for them while they still get to enjoy the item? I sure hope not, otherwise you should have just brought it for them yourself.
2) *Proverbs 22:7 says the borrower becomes servant to the lender.* When you cosign you in essence become a lender because you have lent your good name and credit to someone that makes them a servant to you. Now although people generally don't mind asking for someone to cosign they do tend to resent the same cosigner asking about the status of their loan. But as a cosigner you have a right to know that payments are made on time. Your credit rating is at stake too.
3) *Remember, if they fail to make the payments, their bad payment history will probably show up on your report.* Sometimes the late party is late for months so that when you finally get news of it, the loan may be in collection. This whole procedure will negatively affect your credit rating.
4) *Finally, if you want to keep a good relationship with this person you are considering co signing for, don't do it.* Cosigning has wrecked many a relationships for it allows money to come before friendship, family, etc.

As you can tell, I don't personally approve of cosigning. I have found it to cost me friends and relationships when people fail to make good on their own commitments. Instead, I try to give the money that is needed to make the transaction work if I can afford to. I will help them any way possible but I just refuse to become a business partner with someone who is not capable of holding their own.

This is making credit my servant. So use credit and money wisely to make a better life for yourself.

Money: Servant or Master

Matthew 6:24 – No man can serve two masters

We live in a world that has become increasingly materialistic. In America, we call it the pursuit of the American dream. In reality this dream is just another way of saying we will do whatever is necessary to achieve the goal of having stuff. Now there is nothing wrong with having things and accumulating more. However, it becomes a problem of greed when the motivation to have things supercedes everything else.

Through this dogged determination to have, people have unknowingly made a fatal mistake. In the area of finances, either you will rule them or they will rule you. Many times the pursuit of money has caused people to sacrifice their morals, their family and good judgment all for the sake of a big payday.

Why else would people risk jail for selling illegal drugs? Why would someone risk a good job that involves a high level of trust just to make some extra money? Why would a woman sell her body for cash? All of this is because of the desire to serve the new master, money.

Proverbs 22:7 says the borrower is servant to the lender. Whenever you borrow money from someone you become indebted to him or her. Take buying a house. When you apply to a bank for a loan they allow you to purchase the house by giving you the money. However they don't just make a loan to you. They have you sign a lot of documents that transfer the ownership from the present owner to you. Two standard (though not all the time) documents are the mortgage note and the mortgage.

The mortgage note details the agreement you have to borrow the money. It will tell how much you are borrowing, how much is the principal and interest, and how long you will have to pay the money back. The mortgage describes the security of the loan, the property itself. If you default on the mortgage loan, the lender can call the mortgage due and if you do not pay it, they can foreclose and take the house away from you.

Now if you don't believe that the borrower is servant to the lender, just call the lender up and tell him you think you will not be paying them again. Instead, you will be using your mortgage payment money to bake cookies for all of the kids in the local public school each day. After all, it is your money. Or is it? The lender will probably try to talk some sense into you and if you refuse, they will proceed with the foreclosure proceedings. You can holler and scream all the while but it will not stop the judge from enforcing the lender's right to collect his money. Pretty soon you will have a sheriff escorting you off the LENDER'S PROPERTY because you did not understand that the money you owe makes you a slave until you repay it.

Why do people stay at a dead end job and put up with an abusive boss? Many times it is not because they love their job or their boss but they need the paycheck this job provides. As such, people put up with a lot of abuse from those who hold the purse strings. There is a trap of our modern society; no savings People work more now than ever before and even though they make more money, they own very few items that are free from debt.

It has been said that the average person cannot support themselves from cash reserves for longer than 30 days. This would mean monies held in a checking or savings account, money market or just cash on hand. They would have to tap into their 401 K, IRA or get a home equity loan. We are credit rich and cash poor. It is no wonder people are enslaved to their money; it controls not only their destiny but the destiny of every person in their family as well.

But you say how do we overcome this dilemma? What can we do? After all, it is necessary to save money because I need to have some reserves at my disposal, especially in the case of an emergency. Yes it is very expensive to live. In the city of Chicago where I reside a single person working to provide for their household must earn an above average wage to just get by. It is no wonder that we see both men and women in a family working on a job. Even then, they are usually not living extravagantly but just getting by.

Everybody needs a vacation, right? But the problem is that if you have just enough to live, how will you provide for your vacation? What are you supposed to save when it takes everything to just pay the bills? What ends up happening is instead of saving for a vacation many just finance it. But after coming back from a time of relaxation many are met with overwhelming bills and a bad feeling in the pit of the stomach. We just went to relax and came back to bills.

It is during these times that money becomes valuable. Either it is a servant that is able to help one accomplish worthwhile goals (paying for children's education, a vacation, new car or furniture) and give a sense of fulfillment to the one it serves. Or it is a terrible slave master. If you have too little of it, you must borrow and then pay back. Or for many it means to work yourself to the bone, seeking to have enough to enjoy some parts of your life, even if it is in a limited capacity.

Do you serve money or does it serve you? Ask yourself these questions as a sort of self-quiz;

1) Do you have some of your money invested in vehicles that pay you interest?
2) Do you have money invested in vehicles that are growing in value over time?
3) Are you making the best use of the principle of leverage (where you take

a portion of your money and control an investment many times the size of your down payment, such as purchasing a house, car, etc)?

4) Do you place acquiring money above doing what is right?
5) Do you use money to help people or do you use people with money's help?
6) Do you find yourself doing just about anything for the sake of money?
7) Do you place value on people based on the money they have (Respect the rich and neglect the poor)?

The greatest book ever written (the Bible) has much to say about the subject of money. The books of Proverbs and Ecclesiastes are full of principles that address money and its management.

1) **Proverbs 6:1- 2.** *My son, if you cosign for a friend, if you have entered into an agreement with a stranger; you are snared with the words of your mouth.* To cosign for another person's loan is to agree to make the payments if they do not. The Bible teaches that this is foolish because you have entered into an agreement that binds you and it is usually with a stranger. Instead, if this is the case, do what you can to remove yourself from the legal liability of this loan.

2) **Proverbs 6:6-8** *Go to the ant, oh lazy one. Consider its ways and be wise. For although it has no boss or overseer, yet it stores its provisions in summer and gathers its food in the fall.* Ants are insects that have no boss. Yet they know that you must make money when you are able because if you live long enough, there will come a time when you will not be able to work. This is where you find the principle of saving for retirement. For money to serve us, we must save it, invest it and use it when we need it.

3) **Proverbs 6:10-11** *A little sleep, a little slumber, a little folding of the hands to rest and poverty will come to you like a bandit and scarcity like an armed man.* People who want to make money their servant can't be lazy for poverty creeps up on the lazy person. There is a reward for diligence.

4) **Proverbs 13:11.** *Dishonest money dwindles away but he who gathers money little by little makes it grow.* Most people will never come into a lump sum of money and become rich. Dishonest gains only lead to trouble down the line but a person who makes his money grow little by little will have a guaranteed reward. It allows you to look at your nest egg with a sense of accomplishment because you know it was your hard work that made it grow.

5) **Proverbs 13:22** *A good man leaves an inheritance for his children's children.* A good father wants to bless his children. But a wise father is looking past his children to see how he may bless his grandchildren. Money, properly invested, can be there for these who are your heritage. It also can provide for a college education for your children which will benefit your grandchildren.

6) **Proverbs 14:23** *All hard work leads to profit, but mere talk leads only to poverty.* As I have read on how great men in the past have built great corporations there is one theme that holds true to all of them; hard work. No one gave them much of

anything and they had to persevere to see their dream come to pass. If you want to make money serve you, there must be a willingness to work hard.

7) **Proverbs 22:29** *Do you see a man skilled in his work? He will stand before kings.* When men make money their servant, people of influence begin to take notice of them. Even if you are a general laborer for 30 years but you still save $1,000,000 for retirement on modest wages (which is entirely possible with proper planning), people of means will take notice.

8) **Ecclesiastes 11:4** *whoever watches the wind will not plant and whoever looks at the clouds will not reap.* To make money a servant we must stick to our investment plan. Whenever we are moved by market conditions, current economic status or how much money we have available, we will be hindered. But once we understand the principle of dollar cost averaging (investing money regularly into your plan, regardless of market conditions), we can achieve our goals.

Money should be viewed as a tool. Much like a hammer in the hands of a carpenter who takes pieces of wood and create a masterpiece so too can money accomplish great things in the hands of someone who is skilled at how to use it. Instead of serving money, we must use it like a tool and allow it to serve us. Money can build hospitals, museums, and additions to schools, highways and parks. When we look around and see beauty around us, most of the time it was money that had something to do with it.

This is what makes living our lives solely for the purpose of more money so foolish. Since money is a tool, it is made to be used. Some want to hoard or use it to wield power over others. It's like that old saying, "whoever has the gold rules". But to the person who truly understands the purpose of money, they use it instead of being used by it. Money is not meant to be used to control the destiny of others but rather to make the realization of those destinies possible.

What is the purpose for having money? There are certain things in this life that only money can buy. We need to use it to provide a place to stay, food and clothing. It provides transportation and items necessary for daily living. For many people, money would be the answer to some of the problems they face today. So the purpose of money is to answer life's needs and wants. It is ok to take a nice vacation, live in a nice home and drive a nice car. We can use money to help those less fortunate and to make their standard of living better. Money can actually expose us to the better things in life and stretch the imagination of those who see the better things. It is funny but once you realize there is more to life than what you currently know, it makes life that much bigger.

That being the case, we can never allow money to dictate how the rest of our lives will be run. We should not sacrifice our family for the sake of a bigger and better lifestyle. So many fall into the trap of believing that the only things the people who love them want is what they can buy them. But in most cases, this is not the truth. If a child has to choose between having the top of the line baseball glove or his father at his games, many times the child will choose the father. Now, although it is important to provide, provision must never be our guiding focus in life for a man's life does not consist in the abundance of his possessions.

We must also never allow money to separate us from what is most important to us, our values. Comprising our values cheapens us as people and it is very hard to regain personal value when we sell ourselves so short. No, we must hold fast to what we believe and to the core values that make us who we are.

Understanding its usefulness as a tool, we should use money and love people. Money is neither good nor evil and has no personality. People are the most important for it is only in people that we can have relationships. Have you ever heard of anyone having a tight relationship with his or her wallet (only if they refuse to let it go)? No, we must get away from loving money and using people for if you need a friend to talk to or someone to sit by your hospital bed while you are ill, money can't do that for you.

Now maybe you have never seen yourself as someone who was used by money. Yet all of us are aware of people who serve money, whether they know it or not. For examples, it is not uncommon for a person who sells sex to do so only for money. Without realizing it, they have given themselves to serving money for they would not provide the service unless they get paid. There are people who only work for a paycheck or get into a business deal strictly for the profit.

We need to make sure that we do what we do for reasons other than money. To work to just get paid cheapens your contribution to the organization. It means in essence that you can be brought. We have heard of the horror stories of politicians and city officials on the take, all for the purpose of money. There have even been people who have committed to marry someone they didn't love because of money.

Be a wise master. Let money be your servant. Use it for your own purposes and force it to stay where it deserves, under your control.

Entering the World of Investments

Ecclesiastes 11:1. Cast thy bread upon the water, for you shall find it after many days

Any plan that is going to help you to get your credit situation fixed should include a plan for what to do once you have it fixed. While you are trying to get your finances in order, it is not uncommon to focus so much on debt that there is little thought given to savings and investments. But this is an area where wealthy people excel. Since they don't have to concern themselves with the day-to-day necessities of life (what to eat, where to live, how to cloth their family, etc.) they can focus on investing their wealth and watching it grow.

To begin investing you must first understand the difference between saving money and investing it. When you save, capital preservation (keeping as much of your money as possible) is a high priority. That is why generations past put so much of their money into passbook savings accounts. They were relatively safe and the interest you earned was an added benefit. Personally I have had about 6 savings accounts at different stages in my life. I have never been able to keep one and it took me understanding what it means to invest to tell me why.

Investments are instruments that you use for the sake of growth. They can be in any number of different vehicles (stocks, bonds, real estate, mutual funds, etc.) but the difference between them and traditional savings vehicles (passbook savings accounts, C.D.'s etc) is the rate of return they offer. The rate of return, simply speaking, is how much you earn on your investment. There are many different ways that rate of return can be calculated, depending on which vehicle you are examining.

For example, I have decided personally to strive to do a minimum interest rate in my own investment portfolio. My IRA has been able to do that for some years but I have some mutual funds that have not. These past few years have been pretty bad in generating a good return. It has made many investors change their whole strategy. Since I don't want my whole portfolio held in high-risk vehicles, I have decided to have some more conservative investments that will bring me some balance.

People who invest know that there are a couple of variables that are essential to any investment plan. There is risk, which defines just how much exposure your investment has. Usually the greater the rate of return the higher the level of risk. All investments carry with them some degree of risk or else they are not an investment. You can have a pocket full of thousand dollar bills. The neighborhood you choose to walk in with that kind of money on your person will determine the level of risk associated with the decision to go into that neighborhood. There are certain places you can go and never be questioned about why you are there. But in other neighborhoods, it would definitely not be wise to appear like you have that kind of money in your pocket.

Let me give you some examples of entering the world of investments. I decided at an early age to never let my destiny be controlled by someone else. If I am to fail, I want it to be because I did it, not because some else did it for me. With many of my jobs I had bosses who wanted to limit me and decide just how much I should be paid. I have learned to become the very best that I can in whatever situation I find myself in. When it came to work, I have tried to better myself through specific training and education. I have always wanted to be worth more than I am paid. Then, whenever I needed to discuss money with my employer I could negotiate from a position of strength.

Now the fact of the matter is most of us will never earn enough money from our jobs to truly live at a high level. Everything around us is constantly going up and even when you get pay raise inflation gets a hold of it and makes it less than what you started out with. More income means a higher tax bracket so how do you get ahead in this game of life when there are so many things that bite at your portion of this life.

So I made two decisions. First, I came to realize that I might never be a rich man. Of course this does not mean that I could not be but I refused to have my life center around the pursuit of money and the accumulation of things. Don't misunderstand me, I have had less and I have had more; more is better. If we truly come to understand the covenant God made with man (Abraham, Isaac, Jacob, David, Solomon, Joshua, Moses, etc) it is evident that God never intended for his creation to be in a state of perpetual want. One of his names is JEHOVAH JIREH which means, "Our God will provide". God always provides what we need before the need arrives. That's what makes him such a great father.

There is nothing wrong with having an abundance of this world's goods. The real challenge is being able to balance walking in God's covenant with not worrying about being rich. So the question is, "can we focus on wealth without pursuing it"? That is a real challenge. But if all you do is focus on wealth, you will miss out on the things that money cannot buy.

Money can't buy my children's affection and genuine love. Yes, they love what I can do for them with money but let me let you in on a little secret; when I had no money and was there for my children, they treated me like a king. Money can't buy the love of a good woman; it can't heal a broken heart or heal the despair of a life gone badly. It is true, money cannot buy happiness but it can make misery more bearable.

Since I don't live to be rich, I must make the best of whatever situation I find myself in. That is why is it is so important to do the job you love and just trust that the money will follow. If you are truly good in your chosen field of endeavor, there will be people who are willing to pay for it. Success occurs when preparation runs into opportunity. I cannot always control when an opportunity will present itself but I can prepare myself to be ready when it comes.

The second realization I came to is that it is not so much what you make but what you are able to keep that will determine whether or not you will become truly wealthy. So whatever income I earned I made sure that I did not pay more in income taxes than I legally had to. I saved money looking at what was the best rate of return I could earn, even if it was only $100. I did not waste money even if I came into some extra cash from unexpected sources. Even in the pursuit of our objectives, we should regularly learn to reward ourselves. You need to enjoy today and there were some pleasures you should not deny yourself because we all can use a little pampering.

So work as hard as you can performing a job you really enjoy. Don't buy into the lie that everyone is supposed to be rich, for prosperity will destroy a fool. The truth is there are many of us who cannot handle large sums of wealth. Winners of state lotteries have proven this because many of the winners end up back where they started even though for a season they lived like a millionaire. Instead, grow wise in the world of investments so that you can responsibly manage the assets that come under your control. In the end you will be glad you did. Develop the discipline of saving a little of whatever comes into your hands. Remember, a small amount of money invested over time into a stable investment with a good return will always yield great dividends for you.

Make up your mind to be wealthy (enjoying abundance) in every area of your life. Strive to have and maintain good health. Be content today so that you can enjoy it. Success is not a destination but a journey. Therefore, enjoy the scenery on the ride. You may never have the opportunity to do so again.

Too many people want to blame someone else for their own failures. When we take our future into our own hands and use what we have been given to create what we desire, we have the potential for greatness. No one else can develop your potential but you. If you desire to grow and are willing to pay the price, there will be nothing on this earth that can stop you. Now you may be hindered on your path to success but only you determine whether or not you will be denied.

Let me now give you some practical ways that you can enter into the world of investments;

1) *Understand that we all are either investing our money or spending it.* Investing, in the simplest terms, is to put money in a place where you can end up with more than you started with over a specific period of time. This happens through interest, dividends, capital appreciation, etc. Spending money is just that; once you use it there are no future benefits.
2) *Get on a solid footing first, and then start investing.* When you begin your investment program, don't go back to it to withdraw money. Your goal is to leave it alone and let it grow. Of course, if you ever got in trouble you know that you have this account that you can assess. But it should be treated as a leave alone investment; just because you start to see it grow, don't get happy and go shopping. Develop

the discipline to leave it alone.

3) *Think both short term and long term.* Short term is to have money put aside for unexpected emergencies. You need to have access to some money in the event you need new tires, your furnace goes out or a baseball comes sailing through your back porch window. Long term is the money you have decided beforehand to leave alone. It will be there to provide for your later years.

4) *Take advantage of company sponsored plans.* In many companies they offer profit sharing and 401(k) plans. These can be really helpful in planning your investment strategy. If you are eligible to participate then take advantage of it.

5) *Personal IRA* – these are very good plans for most people. In addition to tax deductibility (in some cases) there is the benefit of having monies grow for you, usually with a good interest rate.

6) *Mutual Funds* – these funds maximize your potential and minimize your risk. They allow you to get into the stock market and have expert assistance.

7) *Take advantage of dollar cost averaging* – learn to save some money every month. Regardless of what you are able to set aside, the discipline alone will help you as you see your nest egg starting to grow.

8) *Become an investor* – Make a decision to invest. There are many different vehicles you can invest in but bottom line, you must become an investor. You will never achieve long-term financial goals unless you develop the discipline to invest. Set aside something.

Remember, anyone can be an investor. Some just have more to invest than others. Even if all you have is a few dollars a week that you put into a savings account earning 2% interest, it is still 2% more than you would have if you didn't save it.

This requires a conscious decision on your part. Many times when we hear the word investor, we think that only people with lots of income can ever become an investor. That is not the way it is today, thanks to the many vehicles we have at our disposal that allow us to invest.

It starts with your thinking. I challenge you to start thinking like someone who has money to invest. Think about how you would be investing your money if all of your bills were paid and there was still something left over. Rich people are not focusing on their needs, they focus on objectives. They set goals and make plans to get there. There is a saying, the poor get poorer and the rich get richer. This has a foundation in the Bible for Luke 16:10 says *"he that is faithful in little will be faithful in much"*. We cannot despise the days of small beginnings for there is no company that is successful and large which started out as big as it is today. Everything healthy grows and our thinking is no exception.

The key is understanding how to make acquiring interest on your investments your best friend. When you make regular deposits into an investment vehicle with a steady interest rate over time, you will most likely end up with more money than you started with. The key is getting started. So many waste precious time because they won't get started.

In 1999 I became part of an Investment Club. 12 people came together and agreed to meet to discuss just what investment options the money we collected as a group would be put into. Each member paid $125 to start to cover all of our initial costs and $50 per month. We contacted a stockbroker and the majority of our money went into the stock market although we also purchased one stock mutual fund. The good thing about this concept is that people who knew very little about investing can come and learned about it along with others. Soon we found ourselves analyzing stocks, reading investment books and magazines and following the stock market closely. We had a very diversified portfolio and we recouped our initial investment and saw our portfolio grow.

What hurt our group is that we were not able to stay together. People moved on, took their proceeds and left the group. Now it's disbanded. In the future, because I do believe in the concept, I will make sure that I do it with people who are committed for the long haul. You cannot build an investment portfolio without a long-term investment focus.

So make a commitment to:

1) Start. Where you are with what you currently have. Begin today.
2) Open a bank Accounts. Most people have one and if not, make sure you do. You need to channel your resources through one avenue and a checking account is an excellent way to start.
3) Commit. Commit to saving a portion each month. Many times people believe that only those with a lot of money can invest. The key is committing to invest a regular portion each month.
4) Look at a mutual fund: You can talk to one of the many investment companies out there and see about opening a mutual fund with them. Many even have the option of investing monthly through a debit from your checking account.
5) Look at stocks. As an individual, you can open your own investment brokerage account and start looking at various stocks. I would suggest you take the time to invest in one of the money magazines on the market and become somewhat knowledgeable at least as to what is going on with some companies. At times, stock investments can be just good old common sense. Typically you would not invest in industries that are not growth oriented. (horses and buggies for transportation is a lost art).
6) Look at real estate. Real Estate can be an excellent option for investing. It has a managerial aspect to it but can be a great way to build solid wealth, if you can devote the resources and time to effectively manage it.

I believe that as you build your investment portfolio, you should strive to not live off it. If you start taking money from your investments before you have accumulated the sum you would like to have, you will severely hinder your plans by eating up your profits prematurely. Now I understand that there are those who use their investments to afford themselves a better lifestyle and there is nothing wrong with that. Investing does not mean that we work and enjoy when we retire. The journey to retirement could use some enjoyment too. Your job needs to pay you enough to meet your current living expenses. If not, then in my opinion, I am not making enough money and need to do something about that.

So don't wait until you are making a lot of money before you start to do something. It is important to put the pieces in place and then make contributions as you are able. Position yourself to have your basic needs taken care of first, and then allocate a certain amount each month for your investment program.

Let's assume that you have only $100 per month that you can invest but you discipline yourself to do it each month for the next 20 years. That means that you will have placed a total of $24,000 into your investment program. Let's also assume that you can earn 10% each year and there is a 5% inflation rate. You would have accumulated a total of $41,374.63, a difference of $17,674.30 that is 73% of what you had originally invested. In other words, your investment grew almost 75% from what you originally started out with. This is the power of investing.

Now using that same example, let's assume you were able to average 12% over that 20 years instead of 10%. Your investment would grow to a total of $52,496.54, a difference of $28,496.54. This would represent 1.18 times more money than you originally invested all because you were able to get 2% more in the interest rate. This is the power of interest.

Come up with a personal definition of what it means to be wealthy to you. This definition of wealth will define how you pursue it. I use to think that wealth meant that one had to be rich. You needed servants, limousines, lots of cash, and visible signs of luxury, a large home, someone who was the envy of the neighborhood. Not only must you have money, you must look like you did.

Now I want to be rich in the things that money can't buy first. It can't buy me the love of my wife or the respect of my children. It can't buy my health and it can't give me strength. If I hate myself, money won't make me love me. It won't give me character, integrity, honesty or dependability. And money alone cannot give me the satisfaction of a job well done.

Don't misunderstand me. There is nothing wrong with visible signs of wealth. If you have it and want to indulge yourself in some of the finer things of life, I don't think it makes you bad because you do. But we need to see that real wealth encompasses a lot more than money and things. It has to include the welfare of people.

Developing an Investment Philosophy

As you progress on your investment journey, develop your own investment philosophy. Why do you need to develop and define your own investment philosophy? Because it will govern how you respond to investment opportunities as you travel on the road to life. It is the foundation for our portfolio. Without it, you will just buy what you hear is good. For example;

1) Will you invest in companies that sell Tobacco? There are those who refuse to do this.
2) How much will you invest in Technology stocks? Will it make up your whole portfolio?
3) How does real estate fit in, if at all?
4) What about cash vehicles (CD', annuities, etc)?

To get free you must start thinking like people who are already free. And once free, work harder to stay free. Remember, if you think you can, you will.

Working Your Plan

Proverbs 24:3-4. Through wisdom is a house built; by understanding it is established and by knowledge shall the chambers be filled with precious and pleasant riches.

As you work to strengthen your financial position, it will require the working out of the plans you have been developing. If there is one problem the average person has, it's not being able to work out their plan even after taking the time to develop it.

Just look at how the average life goes. People enter their early twenties with a lot of dreams. They plan on going to college or learning a trade. They look for just the right job that will offer the right opportunity at the right time. Then when they enter the work force they work and work and work. Then there is more work. As they get older, many become disillusioned, disappointed and discouraged. For all of the hard work, dedication and effort exerted to the advancing of their career, many see a lifetime that will require perpetual struggle.

But there are a select few who face this same scenario but they do so from a different perspective. They understand that no matter who you are working for, in essence you are working for yourself. So they don't put all of their faith in their job or what the potential looks like in their chosen field of endeavor. Instead they make investments into themselves and develop their own potential. This will always prove to be the best investment one can make because no matter what happens to you externally, you will always benefit from personal growth as you continue to grow yourself.

Maybe it is having a business on the side or going into business for yourself. Maybe it is taking a portion of your income and putting it into some investments so that when you retire, your investments can take care of you. Or maybe it is having the courage to live your dream to see it become the outlet for securing your financial future. Whatever the case may be, those who fall into this category are a cut above the rest. For these chosen few have taken their destinies into their hands and their lives will never be the same.

A different perspective

You will never be able to stay focused on your plan looking at your current situation. Sometimes our current situation is very positive and at other times it's negative. But regardless of what we may be facing, we have to see our plan apart from hindrances if we expect it to come to pass. We must position ourselves to dream and this means disassociating with our present situation.

Imagine how discouraging it would be to try to see yourself living a good life, taking vacations all over the country and being in a position to take good care of your family while you are going through a foreclosure and the authorities are coming to set your stuff out on the streets. In this position, you would probably say to yourself, "who am I kidding? This dream will never come to pass for me?"

But if that same person were to first plan how they will come out of that bad immediate situation, they would begin to have hope not only that they will overcome today but that they will be around to fight again tomorrow. A plan must provide a systematic approach that will build the strength of those who follow it by allowing them to have little victories, one at a time.

There was a show on T.V. called "Lifestyles of the rich and famous". Here the world got a chance to see what it was like to be successful and rich. Many lived in dream homes, vacationed at exotic places all over the world, dressed impeccably and earned incomes most of us will never see. In essence, they lived the types of lives many would only dream of.

When you look at successful people you see something that they all have in common if they are not only successful but have been so for awhile; a certain mindset. Successful people see life, others and themselves thru eyes that unsuccessful people are clueless about.

They believe that life affords one an opportunity to prosper. Some did not come from a famous family or even have wealth as a child. But they grew up and believed that they could make it in this world and make it big. *Do you believe that the greatest gift any of us have is the power to choose to take advantage of a given situation?* There are chances and opportunities before us all. The wise person knows when to build their dreams.

This country affords everyone the right to dream. But once a dream has been realized, it takes a plan. Plans require effort to develop and even more effort to make it happen. In this plan there needs to be certain components which will be necessary for future success;

1) *Define the goal:* Just as in football there is an end zone with a large marker to tell all where it is at, so too there must be a destination for our plan. We must answer the question, "where am I going and what will it look like once I get there?" So many times people have plans that do not coincide with their goals and then they wonder why they fail to get there. So at the beginning, define what the goal is and make sure the plan will get us there.

2) *Set a realistic time to work the plan*: There is a reason why it typically takes 4 years to get a college degree. Now although one may be able to get one in less time, to think that one can go to college today and get a degree by tomorrow afternoon is unrealistic. Our plans must have a realistic time frame. To do that we must determine just how much time it will take to accomplish certain tasks. Then we must work to adhere to that time frame so as to not throw the rest of our plan off by having too many delays.

3) *Predetermine what resources you will need to work your plan:* There will always be a need to have resources to reach goals. It takes something to create something. So when we make our plans, we need to see what we will need (people, finances, tools, etc) in order to make the dream a reality.

4) *Pay attention to the plan.* Once the plan has been implemented, someone will need to pay attention to the details of the plan. This is why most New Years Resolutions never work. In December the plan is made, in January it is implemented and by March the plans are not being followed. Many times people don't review the plans until December, where the cycle starts all over again.

5) *Reward yourself along the way.* Nothing is harder to do than maintaining momentum for something that one day will be. We need to have periodic stops that allow us to review our forward progress. When we see that we are moving, a small reward is in order. It may be a treat to an ice cream parlor or taking a stroll along a flowery path. But whatever we decide to do, remember that positive motivation works wonders.

6) *When the plan has finally been realized, bring it to a close.* Maybe your plan is so good that you see it is working beyond your wildest expectations. Remember, no one can function at a high intensity level forever. This will mean that even if your plan is a great one, it needs to come to an end. This will allow you to savor the victory and prepare for the next battle you might need to engage in.

It always helps to have someone on your side, someone who believes in you. This is especially true when we think about our plans.

The Rewards of Diligence

Proverbs 22:29 – Do you see a man diligent in his work? He shall stand before kings.

No matter how good a plan might be, if it is void of diligence, it is destined for failure. To get from point A (the point of origin, where we all begin) to point B (our desired destination) will require diligence.

Diligence is the ability to stick to something until it is completed. It allows one to continue on in the face of adversity for adversity is a reality in the day in which we live. To think that success will come without obstacles is foolish. But diligent people press on and keep their eyes focused in front of them.

To better understand this principle of diligence, one needs look into the world of sports to watch it displayed. In high school I ran track and since I was not a fast runner, I did the distance runs. I remember the coach giving me some pointers on winning races;

1) *Understand that this is not a race of speed, but one of endurance.* He told me that since I had a long way to go (usually miles) it was not wise to start off running as fast as I can. Instead I would need to pace myself for if I gave it all I had in the beginning, there would be nothing left for the end. Life is like that. It's not a sprint but a marathon.

2) *Stay focused.* Don't pay attention to the runner on the right or the left. He said if I focused on what was going on around me (how far ahead of the rest of the group I was, how far behind I was of the leader of the group) that I might get over confident or discouraged. In life, we need to stop trying to keep up with the Joneses.

3) *Keep the goal in front of you.* So many times in a race we see everything but the one thing we are supposed to look at, the finish line. It is impossible to focus on more than one thing with undivided attention. Instead, I needed to focus on the prize that was before me which was the finish line.

4) *Encourage yourself along the way.* It helps to talk to yourself while you run so that you can encourage yourself. Many times in a race, there is no one to talk to. If left alone, our minds will wander so by encouraging oneself, it is possible to stay focused for the duration of the race. As we live out our lives, we can stay in the race by telling ourselves we are doing a good job.

5) *When you see the finish lines (goal) go for it with everything you have.* In track we called it the second wind. It was the time when you saw the finish line before you and you pushed with everything you had left to make it across the line. Many times runners who developed this had such a second wind you would have thought they had not just finished running a track race. In life, we can never quit and we must refuse to give up. As we see the goals we have been working for suddenly within our reach, we must go after them with everything we have.

Diligence requires steady progress. It is not the fastest, smartest or the strongest who usually wins, just the one with the most diligence. It requires stick – to – it – ness. Like fly trapped on flypaper, once a project has been started, it must be finished.

One of the qualities that followers like to see in their leaders is steadfastness. No one likes to follow someone who is up today and down tomorrow. Followers want to feel like their leader will stick to their decision and follow through on their commitments.

Never, ever quit

During the time that diligence is being developed, there is an attitude that must be cultivated with it; that is the determination to never, ever quit.

Life and circumstances will present many reasons as to why quitting would be the ideal thing to do. It may be too hard to continue; there may not be any real solution to the problems that you face; or maybe, it could be that since quitting is easier, it is the ideal route to take at this time.

But quitting is the opposite of diligence. It is the one trait that all failures have in common; at some point, they just quit, gave up. No one who ever experiences true success does so by quitting. There is an old saying that quitters never win and winners never quit. This is certainly proven true when it comes to achieving lasting financial success.

Everyone who ever desires to do anything worthwhile with his or her life will face challenges. It is not the presence of challenges that defeats us but rather the tendency to give up because we are challenged. When we can accept challenges as a way of life then we can cease to see challenges as the final outcome but rather necessary steps in the achieving of our goals.

People who are diligent overcome; they find a way to see an answer because they are looking for it. It is amazing but once you quit, you cease to look for answers. Instead we start planning the funeral, making final arrangements for our inevitable demise. But the diligent continue to look. They open up their mind to options and possibilities. A problem exists because no one has discovered the answer but many things that were problems yesterday are no longer problems today. Somebody discovered an answer.

People who are diligent feel good about themselves; there is just something very satisfying about looking at the answer to a problem that you helped to solve. Once you get a chance to view things from the other side, there is a sense of satisfaction that comes upon you. As a people we are very competitive and this trait comes in handy when one is trying to overcome financial adversity.

People who are diligent go on to bigger and tougher problems; it's like purchasing real estate. That first house represents a major hurdle to property ownership. Once you pick up that first investment piece, it's not too hard to see the second one. Or the 3rd. When we attack little problems and overcome them, it paves the way to solving larger problems.

This is the principle necessary to understand if your ultimate desire is to accomplish great things. There must be a string of victories that you can look back to so that you can have faith to believe that it is possible. The Bible tells the story of David and Goliath (I Samuel 17). One of the reasons David could face the giant Goliath who stood over 9 feet tall was that David had previously defeated a lion and a bear while he was a shepherd over his father's sheep. Because he could reference prior smaller victories, he had the faith to believe that this giant who stood before him would be as one of them. He took that faith into battle and won the victory for his people. However, it was not his victory over the lion or the bear that paved the way for him to serve in the king's palace. It was his victory over Goliath. But without the lion and bear, he never would have defeated Goliath and may never have gained the respect of the people he would one day lead.

That is why it is so important to win. Winning is not the only thing but it is the necessary thing. I do not believe in winning at any cost. There cannot be a compromising of values when it comes to winning. But winning in any area of your life will set you up to win in every area of your life. You see people who win have a great attitude about difficulties. They don't see them as obstacles but opportunities.

When's the last time you heard of a seminar entitled "12 *ways to fail in business. Or six ways to never recover from a setback? How about guidelines for a loser?"* The reason we never see these types of seminars is that people don't pay to learn how to lose. They do that just fine without anyone's help. What they want to know is how do we win? How can I overcome difficult situations and come out on top? This is a valid request for we are not equipped to handle perpetual failure. People in general want to win.

How many times have parents said they want their children to end up on drugs, in jail, or as socially unfit misfits? No good parent wishes that on his or her child. On the contrary, they want them to be social examples, pillars in the community, role models and people that others can look up to. Not only do they want to succeed themselves, they want their children to as well. That is why there is so much sacrifice and dedication to child development. We want them to develop into something we can be proud of.

In the same way, you will never develop to your full potential if you quit when it gets tough. Let's face it, it gets tough for everyone but that never stopped the one who was determined to make something worthwhile out of their life.

You can fix whatever you face. Just decide to not give up *"until you fix it"*.

Once Out, Then What

John 8:11 neither do I condemn thee; go and sin no more.

Now we are nearing the end of our journey. We have spoken of assessing our current situation, making a plan, understanding and using credit, money and investments along with diligence. But what happens once we are out? What happens when the financial pressure subsides and we can see daylight again?

First, let me say that if you focus on coming out with a good plan and persistence, you will one day see the other side. At times it seems dark in the middle but just hold on. As sure as day follows night, night will follow day as well.

But when you get to the other side, there are some principles you will need to apply if you wish to stay out.

1) *The goal is not to just get out of debt or be financially free; the goal is to live in such a way as to never be in bondage again.* Getting free can't be enough for you. It is like people who work to overcome addictions. They can't focus just on stopping the usage of drugs. They must have a plan so that when they are tempted to repeat bad habits (and they will be tempted) to replace them with the new habits they learned on the road to recovery. The same is true of overcoming financial problems. If we don't replace new learned behavior and habits for the old ones that got us in trouble, it is very likely that we will repeat those bad habits again. Take it from a man who has seen his share of financial difficulties more than once. This mindset has helped me stay free even in adversity.

2) *Learn to follow success.* I try to read books of successful people so that I can learn how they addressed the problems that they face. I know that in order for them to remain successful, they must have a way of looking at and addressing their problems. I want to know what makes them different than the rest of us. In addition, I try to surround myself with people who either have something or are moving towards it. Failure can only bring birth to failure but success is the environment for more success.

3) *Learn the value of helping others.* One of the most discouraging things I have ever had to overcome was that there was no one to help me. When I approached people in the business world who were more successful than I with my plans of becoming more successful, some would laugh and others would patronize me. But very few would embrace a young man with big ideas, big dreams and bigger visions. Borrowing money was out of the question. When I first tried to get into real estate investing, I had no money, no credit and no help. It was incredibly hard to make things happen. Now I had taken many real estate courses on different ways to buy and I was well versed in finance. But let me tell you, it takes money to make money. That is why the rich get richer and the poor get poorer. In order to prosper, you must have something to work with.

This is one of the reasons why I understand how important it is to help others. As you begin to walk in true financial freedom, think of more than yourself or your family. There is a single mom that could use a hand up or a father with a high school education who might find it hard to make ends meet. There are countless people that successful people can reach out to and help. Notice, I didn't say reach down to, I said reach out. Even when you are struggling, you don't want to feel like a charity case. No, let us help everyone maintain some dignity and treat them as equals. I know this may be hard for some egos to swallow but imagine if it were you in need of help. How would you feel if your help treated you in a condescending manner? Respect is necessary to achieve great things in this world.

4) *Help your community.* There is just something about giving. We need to make a contribution to the community we live in. Maybe it is volunteering at our local church and getting into ministry. Or joining the local school board. Maybe it is agreeing to coach little league or tee ball. Whatever the contribution, when you are free financially, give back so that others can become empowered to give as well. Successful people need to be examples to all those that they can exercise some influence with.

5) *Find someone whom you can personally mentor, one on one.* I like to pour out what I have been given to another person who also has dreams. All successful people perpetuate their success by having a successor (that is why many times when a man starts a business, he trains his children to take over when he retires). This means I take time to meet with them and we talk philosophy. But I don't like to waste time, particularly on people who will not yield a profitable return on the investment of time made. In other words, don't mentor people who have no interest in becoming your student. If they don't want to learn from what you can teach them, leave them alone. Let them find someone else to waste their time with. Your time is too valuable and there are too many willing candidates for you to be delayed by someone who ultimately will be a waste of time.

6) *Never stop learning.* Remain a lifelong student. Whenever you think you have arrived, you are in trouble. A wise person realizes that success is a journey, not a destination. You will never get done being successful. You will only grow in your efforts to become successful. Your influence may grow. Your knowledge and understanding may grow. But you must never stop growing. And we grow when we learn. So whatever your trade is, perfect it. Whatever your gifts are, learn how to better yourself.

7) *Give and it shall be given to you.* There is something lasting about giving. Successful people give of their time (through volunteering), treasures (those things that they possess and others want), and talents (the skills which they have). They make contributions to worthy causes. They support those things they believe in and their wealth affords them the opportunity to do some great things.

I truly believe that when the purpose of success is understood, people strive to get free so that they can help others. Just imagine how this world would be if the famous inventors of old only used their discoveries for their own families and loved ones? The majority of us would have missed out because we all didn't have inventors in our families. No, what they did was share what they discovered. They made it available to all of us and today we all benefit. That is how we need to view success. Let the masses benefit from what you have accomplished. Success is not only meant to be enjoyed, it is meant to be shared.

The world needs to have more models of people who have learned how to handle true success. I am not talking about just being successful in one area, such as money, but to truly experience success in all areas. We see around us today people who have plenty of money and fame but they cannot keep their families together. Their children end up being the product of a broken home and all the money in the world can't fix that.

Or they become settlers in their relationship. These are those people who are really unhappy in their relationship but because of the financial rewards they receive, they stay in it. Their marriage has become a marriage of convenience because it is the most prudent thing for them to do at this point in their life. What we need are more people who have the money they need to live productive lives and yet have other things in life that money cannot buy: a good home, someone who loves them on this earth for them, a cause worth living and dying for, etc.

Use your freedom to reach others and watch how much more you will have in return.

Personal Commitments

Let me end this book with some closing thoughts on commitments I believe you need to make to yourself and others as you begin this journey.

Remember, people who have been strapped by debt need to work to enjoy the freedom that can be theirs. This will require a change of thinking and a change of focus.

1) **Never trade people for things**. Always remember that people matter and are irreplaceable. Things on the other hand break and can be replaced. Never forget the value of a human being.
2) **Commit to stay focused.** Don't forget where you are going. People continually miss their destiny by looking at the wrong things at the right time. Your success journey is like a trip to the grocery store on Main St. If you go down Delay Drive you will miss your stop. Focused commitment will be the key to your breakthrough.
3) **Love somebody other than yourself.** Selfless love, the type that commits to another is essential for lasting success. As long as you are the most important person in your world you will be very selfish.
4) **If you are married, then make this a family commitment.** I cannot stress this enough. Don't sacrifice your spouse and children for monetary success. No matter what you gain to lose your family, the price is too high. Let them know that their emotional stability and well-being is paramount in your goals. Don't let them come to hate you because of your neglect.
5) **Teach your children as you have been taught**. Don't perpetuate ignorance. If you have learned some things that have made your life easier, share them with your children. Teach them the value of helping others. Let them help others as others have helped you.
6) **No matter how successful you become, always remember that success is the byproduct of providing something for someone**. Trade goods and / or services for what you desire in your own life.
7) **Let others help you to remain humble while successful.** Humility is a great trait for successful people to have for it makes them approachable and reachable.
8) **Never stop learning.** Remember you have not arrived, you have just left. Make a commitment to add to your learning wisdom, which is the application of knowledge.
9) **Learn to be grateful**. So many times we think that everything good we have we deserve and nothing is farther from the truth. It is good to remember that everyone who suffers does not suffer because they deserve to. When we have been given much, we should thank much. May we always give honor and thanksgiving to the one who has made all this possible.

"I want to spend my life helping hurting people"

This quote speaks to the desires of Dr. Jeff Davis. My goal is to reach people with truth and help them to walk in victory in every area of their lives.

Dr. Jeff holds a Doctorate in Theology and has spent years counseling married couples along with working with premarital couples.

He has held licenses in Real Estate and Insurance in various states. He has owned and operated Real Estate Investment companies.

Visit the following websites for more info;

www.drjeffknows.wordpress.com

www.lordshipinc.com

www.ezinearticles.com

Look on Kindle and Amazon for more books by Dr. Jeff on the subjects of marriage, family, real estate and investing.

www.ingramcontent.com/pod-product-compliance
Lightning Source LLC
Chambersburg PA
CBHW081221170526
45165CB00009B/2904